WORLD'S GREATEST LEADERS

●

THE
AKENS
BOOK
OF
SUPERNATURAL
RECORDS

By David Akens

THE STRODE PUBLISHERS
HUNTSVILLE, ALABAMA 35801

To Aunt Adah and Uncle George, and to
mother and father, who—on a river of found
faith—helped establish a school for orphans at
Lost Creek, Kentucky, U.S.A.

Grateful Acknowledgment For The Use Of Photographs Is
Made To Art Institute Of Chicago; Association For Research
And Enlightenment, Edgar Cayce Foundation; Belgian National
Tourist's Office; Christian Broadcasting Network; The Christian
Science Publishing Society; Cleveland Museum Of Art; Embassy
Of Japan; Government Of India Information Services; Govern-
ment of India Tourist Office; *Hindustan Times*; International
Church Of The Foursquare Gospel, Raymond L. Cox; Kathryn
Kuhlman Foundation, Maggie Hartner; National Monuments
Record; Oral Roberts University; Trans World Airlines; Union
Of American Hebrew Congregations; United Press International;
Unity School Of Christianity; University of Utrecht; Wheaton
College.

Contents

Note

Guidance in preparation of this book may or may not have been supernatural. Vacation at an isolated south Alabama lodge featured discovery of elusive books about Kathryn Kuhlman and about yoga. The only full-face volume on the book shelves of an agnostic, who professes belief in nothing supernatural, was a scarce and helpful volume related to supernatural experiences. Coincidences? Possibly. Yet unusually helpful.

Another thing. This book does not attempt to either justify or tear apart the claims to the following records. Above all it does not attempt to "sit in the seat of the scornful." It includes records in which thousands of people believe. There is no attempt to risk the wrath of the gods by questioning the beliefs of many thousands. That is left for those with either more courage or less knowledge.

All the following material comes from printed or written records. Most helpful has been research at public and private libraries and correspondence with individuals and institutions. Each report assumes the viewpoint of the eyewitness. Of course, what is supernatural to one may be altogether natural to another.

It is interesting that of the seven major historic religions—Buddhism, Confucianism, Hinduism, and Taoism in the East and Christianity, Islam, and Judaism in the West—miracles are most associated with Buddhism, Hinduism, Christianity, and Judaism. Of these four religions, Christianity more than any other rests its case on a single pivotal miracle, the ability to rise from the dead.

Rather than major historic religions, Africa and the American Indians have had thousands of diversified, smaller religious groups. Although belief in supernatural happenings has been a hallmark among Africans and American Indians, from dire voodoo to Happy Hunting Grounds, there is not enough focus to feature individual supernatural African or American Indian events. If one can pardon a pun, a research of supernatural records in those areas reveals too many Indians and not enough chiefs. Hence their omission in this book.

Please note, too, that this book's title is *World's Greatest Leaders* rather than *All The World's Greatest Leaders*. The compiler of this work is painfully aware that there are many more supernatural world record holders omitted from this initial representative volume. If it is to be, later editions will add to the number recorded from throughout the universe.

Oh, yes—a word about the word supernatural. Maybe we need a contest to choose the proper word. Supernormal? Extrasensory? Paragnosis (beyond knowledge)? Clairvoyant? Psychic? Paranormal? The word supernatural may have been with us far too long in a world where the supernatural is becoming natural. But can any alternate word not be dated in the face of expanding supernatural knowledge? After all, we are no longer limited to such questions as, "How high is the moon?"

Altering World Events Through Mind Direction

SRI AUROBINDO (A.D. August 15, 1872-December 5, 1950). India. Calcutta.

Born to an affluent environment the child was named Aurobindo Ghose. Dr. Ghose, his father, sent Aurobindo at the age of seven to England to study under a tutor. He entered St. Paul's school in London, where he was a brilliant student, excelling in six different languages. After 14 years in England he returned to India and became vice-principal of Baroda College. His fame spread as a scholar and writer and as an activist in worthwhile causes. On one occasion he declared to his wife that he had three mighty convictions: though the world might call him mad, he must give all his possessions to his needy countrymen because his possessions were only in trust given him from God; he must see God face to face; and he must help free India from British control. This third goal led to his arrest by the British and the accomplishment of his second goal, for in the seclusion of his prison cell he had a vision of Sri Krishna. The vision enveloped him with the complete desire to learn spiritual truth, an important part of his search becoming the practice of Yoga.

After a year the British government released Aurobindo, and from 1910 until his death in 1950 he made Pondicherry the headquarters of his search for religious truth. Many disciples gathered around him in this religious community he established. His fame became so great one of the devotees who came to worship and serve under Aurobindo was Margaret Wilson, the daughter of United States President Woodrow Wilson. Though after seven years she became critically ill, she refused to return to the United States for traditional medical treatment, saying that if she died here her soul would be in divine hands but elsewhere it might not.

Sri Aurobindo never left Pondicherry after his arrival in 1910, and for the last 25 years of his life he retired to his living quarters "for the purposes of spiritual growth." But from this seclusion he used what he and his disciples called his "Force" to drastically alter world events. Though a recluse he kept a number of international journals as well as daily papers beside him. He had a radio installed in his room and spent several hours daily listening to world news. During World War II he felt that the fate of humanity rested on the outcome of the war. Except for five and six hours, day and night, he worked for victory by the Allies. He directed his Force to help Churchill, whom he greatly admired, and against Hitler, whom he considered the embodiment of evil. His Force drastically affected the outcome of the war.

A noteworthy example of Force against Hitler was the irrational behavior of Hitler at the time of Dunkirk. He failed to heed the urgent advice of his generals to push the Allies back into the channel. They considered Hitler insane when he insisted that his air force alone could destroy the invaders. Because of Hitler's untenable decision, the Allied forces were able to escape destruction. Sri Aurobindo's Force caused Hitler to avoid the decision that would have destroyed the Allies.

In addition to changing world affairs, Sri Aurobindo also performed hundreds of acts of healing, regardless of the physical distance between him and the patient. Even when the time came to leave his physical body, Sri Aurobindo used his psychic Force to affect his own physical health. In India, before the advent of embalming, body decomposition would set in within a few hours. But after his physical death on December 5, 1950, his disciples saw a concentration of supramental light and for the ensuing 90 hours his psychic Force was still enough in control to prevent decomposition. Even after that time, when his body was laid to rest in a tomb in the courtyard, he held a conversation with the disciple he left in charge of the religious community. The disciple asked Sri Aurobindo why he did not resuscitate his own body. He responded that he had left his body on purpose and did not wish to take it back. But that he would return again at a later time in a more spiritually advanced form.

His disciples feel that Sri Aurobindo continues to be present among them, even though he has left his physical body. Many report having seen him and talking with him, particularly when near his tomb. Numerous devotees gather twice weekly to worship at Pondicherry.

Sri Aurobindo grew up in an India where the supernatural is so commonplace it seems natural to millions. Here Hindu faithful gather along the Ganges River to wash away their sins and obtain a better life in future incarnations.

Annihilating Nature's Laws

MOSES (circa 1200 B.C.). Egypt. Perhaps Akhetaton (present-day Tell el-Amarna).

God had spared Isaac from being killed by his father, and Isaac grew to manhood and fathered a son Jacob. Jacob fathered a son, Joseph, who at age 17 was sold by his jealous half-brothers and ended as a slave on the Pharoah's staff in Egypt. This entry of Joseph into Egypt led to many Jewish descendants there, and not quite halfway in overall Jewish history between Abraham and Jesus Christ there was born in Egypt a baby named Moses. It was during a time of great persecution of the Jews in Egypt under a new Pharoah who feared that if "war breaks out, they [the Jews] will join our enemies and fight against us and escape out of the country" (Exodus 1:10). The Pharoah ordered the Jews enslaved under brutal taskmasters. When this failed to alleviate his fears, he ordered the killing of all the Hebrew boys by throwing them into the Nile as soon as they were born. A Jewish couple in the Levi tribe had a baby boy whose mother managed to hide him for three months on land and then decided to hide him among the reeds along the river's edge in a little boat made from papyrus reeds waterproofed with tar. The baby's older sister then set up a watch from the distance until one of the Pharoah's daughters, a princess, came down to bathe in the Nile. Discovering the crying child, the princess' heart was touched, and when the baby's older sister approached and suggested that a Hebrew nurse could nurse the baby, if the princess would keep him, the princess

10

agreed. Some of the family intelligence that the baby himself would show in later years now came to light as the older sister hurried off and brought back the boy's real mother to nurse her own baby for the princess. The baby was given the name Moses, meaning "to draw out;" and after taking him home and nursing him, the real mother returned him to the Pharoah's household where he became the princess' son.

When Moses was grown he went out one day to visit his fellow Hebrews; seeing an Egyptian knock a Hebrew to the ground, Moses killed the Egyptian. Hearing that Pharoah had ordered his arrest and execution for this, Moses escaped to the land of Midian, where he was taken into the home of the priest of Midian and married one of the priest's daughters. Then one day while out tending flock for his priest father-in-law Moses saw a burning bush that would not burn up. When he went over to investigate, God called out of it to him, "I have seen the deep sorrows of my people in Egypt, and. . .I am going to send you to Pharoah to demand that he let you lead my people out of there." But Moses objected that even his own Hebrew people in Egypt would not believe him. "They won't do what I tell them to. They'll say, 'Jehovah never appeared to you,'" he said. So the Lord asked him, "What do you have there in your hand?" Moses replied, "A shepherd's rod." Whereupon the Lord told him, "Throw it down on the ground," and when Moses did, it became a serpent and Moses ran from it. Then the Lord told him, "Grab it by the tail!" He did, and it became a rod in his hand again. "Do that and they will believe you!" the Lord told him. For good measure the Lord added, "Now reach your hand inside your robe, next to your chest." When Moses did and removed his hand again it was white with leprosy. "Now put it in again," Jehovah said. And when Moses did, and took it out again, "it was normal just as before." (Exodus 4:7).

So 80-year-old Moses accompanied by his 83-year-old brother Aaron went to the Pharoah in Egypt, and to add credence to God's demand to free the Hebrews, God asked Aaron to throw down a rod which became a serpent before Pharoah and his court. But Pharoah countered by calling in his sorcerers —the magicians of Egypt—and they were able to do the same thing with their magical arts! So, even though Aaron's serpent swallowed their serpents, Pharoah continued his harsh oppression of the Hebrew people. Next God told Moses to have Aaron waiting when Pharoah came to the Nile the following morning, whereupon Aaron, as Pharoah and all of the officials watched, hit the surface of the Nile with the rod and the river turned to blood. Aaron also pointed the rod toward all the waters of Egypt: all its rivers, canals, marshes, and reservoirs, and even the water stored in bowls and pots in the homes turned to blood. But though the fish died and the water stank and there was no drinking water in the land until the Egyptians dug wells, in turn the magicians of Egypt used their secret arts to turn water into blood and Pharoah remained unswerving. Then the Lord said to Moses, "Instruct Aaron to point the rod toward all the rivers, streams, and pools of Egypt, so that there will be frogs in every corner of the land," and though Aaron did, and frogs covered the nation, the magicians did the same and Pharoah remained unchanged. Even when Aaron next struck the dust with his rod, and lice covered all of Egypt, and even though this time the magicians could not duplicate the feat, the Pharoah remained steadfast. Next came a devastating plague of flies, so devastating that Pharoah agreed this time to let the people go. Except that as soon as the flies departed Pharoah changed his mind. Next God sent a plague that destroyed all the cattle, horses, donkeys, camels, flocks, and herds in Egypt, except those belonging to the Israelites; and as Pharoah remained unrelenting, the next plague consisted of boils that broke out throughout all Egypt. The boils in fact were so painful, even the magicians themselves could not stand before Moses. Next came a "terrible beyond description" hailstorm that pommeled Egypt except for the Israelites. Next came a thick layer of locusts that covered the land and destroyed everything still standing. This was followed in turn by darkness without a ray of light upon all the land of Egypt.

Finally Moses quoted Jehovah to Pharoah, saying, "About midnight I will pass through Egypt, and all the oldest sons shall die in every family in Egypt, from the oldest child of Pharoah, heir to his throne, to the oldest child of his lowliest slave; and even the firstborn of the animals." Then the Lord had Moses and Aaron announce to the Israelites that they should kill lambs "and their blood shall be placed on the two side-frames of the door of every home and on the panel above the door. . . . The blood you have placed on the doorposts will be proof that you obey me, and when I see the blood I will pass over you and I will not destroy your firstborn children when I smite the land of Egypt." The Israelites were to eat bread made without yeast, were to eat rapidly, and with "your traveling clothes on, prepare for a long journey. . . ."

The Hebrews followed the Lord's instructions for the "passover" and the Pharoah did not. Agonized by the resultant terrible calamity across the land, Pharoah and the Pharoah's officials and the Egyptian people alike gave in. They even donated to the Hebrews all the silver and gold jewelry and clothing they wanted, and as a result "the Egyptians were practically stripped of everything they owned. . . . That night the people of Israel left Rameses and started for Succoth; there were six hundred thousand of them, besides all the women and children, going on foot." (Exodus 12:37). The Lord guided them by a pillar of cloud during the daytime, and by a pillar of fire at night. But the Pharoah pursued the people of Israel, for not only were they removing themselves from his service they were taking much of the wealth of Egypt with them. Pharoah led the chase in his chariot, followed by the pick of Egypt's chariot corps—600 chariots in all—and other chariots driven by Egyptian officers. Ahead lay the Red Sea. Behind them the Egyptians were closing in. But "Moses stretched his rod over the sea, and the Lord opened up a path through the sea, with walls of water on each side; and a strong east wind blew all that night, drying the sea bottom. So the people of Israel walked through the sea on dry ground!" Then the Egyptians followed them between the walls of water along the bottom of the sea—all of Pharoah's horses, chariots, and horsemen. But with the Israelites safely across, the Lord said to Moses, "Stretch out your hand again over the sea, so that the waters will come back over the Egyptians and their chariots and horsemen." And so, of all the army of Pharoah that chased after the Israelites through the sea, not one remained alive, and the people of Israel saw the Egyptians dead, washed up on the seashore.

Though the children of Israel under Moses now wandered 40 years in the wilderness after crossing the Red Sea, the Lord gave them drinking water from the ground or from rock and food from the skies as needed. The food that the Lord provided

13

became known as "manna," meaning "What is it?" It was white, like coriander seed, and flat, and tasted like honey bread. During the wilderness trek, if Israel started losing a battle with warring tribes Moses simply would lift up the same rod that had done such wonders, including the parting of the Red Sea, and the ebb of battle would change in favor of the Israelites. Yet beyond what had happened until now, it was a series of events that occurred three months after the night of their departure from Egypt that has given Moses a preeminence in the Old Testament suggestive of Christ's in the New. Upon arriving at the base of Mt. Sinai, the Israelites established camp there. Moses climbed the mountain to talk with God, beginning a series of conversations including messages relayed by God down to the people waiting below. On the morning of the third day there was a great storm and a cloud upon the mountain and a long, loud blast as from a ram's horn. While all the people trembled Mt. Sinai was covered with smoke billowing into the sky as from a furnace as Jehovah descended in the form of fire, the mountain shaking with a violent earthquake and the trumpet blast growing louder and louder. God's voice thundered, calling Moses to the top of the mountain, and Moses ascended to God. There God instructed him in great detail in what has become known as the Mosaic Law. Then, as God finished speaking with Moses on Mount Sinai, he gave him two tablets of stone on which the Ten Commandments were written with the finger of God.

As the Israelites wandered 40 years in the wilderness, eating the manna from heaven for the full 40 years until they arrived in Canaan, it was God's law carved in stone and followed by multitudes that was the greatest miracle in the life of Moses. (Quotes related to the lives of Abraham, Moses, Jesus, and Paul come from *The Living Bible Paraphrased*, Tyndale House Publishers, 1971.)

Twenty-eight centuries after Moses led a migration of his people to Canaan, shattering nature's laws en route, followers of his Hebraic religion continued to emigrate and prosper. Here is a pioneering synagogue in North America, built in Newport, Rhode Island, in 1658 by a group of Portuguese-Spanish Sephardi Jews.

15

The account of Moses is prominent in this Torah. It contains the first five books of the Bible, called the Pentateuch, considered by the Hebrews the Bible's most holy part.

From the time of Moses the blowing of a ram's horn has marked high religious observances among the Hebrews.

Blinding Light Alters
World History

PAUL THE APOSTLE (circa 1 B.C.-?). The Roman city of Tarsus, at the time an east-west crossroads city between Egypt and the Euphrates valley.

His Hebrew parents named their child Saul. He had the advantage of being born in a prominent Roman city of unusual learning and culture with a history going back to about 4000 B.C. No one is certain when Saul obtained the second name of Paul, though probably it was in honor of someone Saul or his family admired. Historians have long conjectured that in his early teens Saul went to live with his sister in Jerusalem and there became a student of a strict Pharisee who not only taught him the Hebrew religion but Greek literature as well. Although Saul was born at about the same time as Jesus Christ, and possibly was in Jerusalem between the years A.D. 26 and A.D. 30, historians seem generally to doubt that Saul had known Jesus prior to the Resurrection.

Certainly the actions of Saul of Tarsus during Christ's lifetime and for two or three years after the Resurrection showed anything but Christian influence. Instead, Saul became a fanatical leader of one of two schools of thought that sprouted in Christ's latter years and blossomed and bore fruit with Christ's Crucifixion and Resurrection. One school maintained that Christ was a fake and that he was anything but the Messiah so long awaited by the Jews. It was followers of this school of thought who crucified Christ. Until after the Crucifixion and Resurrection one of the most rabid zealots of this school was Saul of Tarsus. The other school agreed with Jesus that indeed he was

17

the Son of God, born by immaculate conception, and that his widely witnessed and discussed miracles were because of his divine sonship. Saul's side of the controversy seemed to gain ascendance with the Crucifixion but then was met head-on by the fact that Christ reappeared physically to 70 or more people on various occasions for a period of 40 days after the Crucifixion. And then a number of witnesses observed his final ascent from the Mount of Olives into a cloud (Acts 1-15).

The reports of witnesses to Christ's Resurrection, plus a remembrance of Christ's own resurrection predictions, plus the Christlike miracles that Christ's followers themselves now began performing, began bringing in an increasing number of disciples. Among the new disciples was Stephen, a "man so full of faith and the Holy Spirit's power" that he "did spectacular miracles among the people." (Acts 6:8). In addition Stephen accused those who refused to become Christians as being "stiff-necked heathen . . . . The Jewish leaders were stung to fury by Stephen's accusation, and ground their teeth in rage." They led a mob that "dragged him out of the city [of Jerusalem] to stone him. The official witnesses—the executioners—took off their coats and laid them at the feet of a young man named Paul [Saul of Tarsus]. And as the murderous stones came hurtling at him, Stephen prayed, 'Lord Jesus, receive my spirit.' And he fell to his knees, shouting 'Lord, don't charge them with this sin!' and with that he died. Paul was in complete agreement with the killing of Stephen . . . . Paul was like a wild man, going everywhere to devastate the believers, even entering private homes and dragging out men and women alike and jailing them." (Acts 7:51-8:3).

With unabated anti-Christian zeal Paul, probably during the era A.D. 33-36, and "threatening with every breath and eager to destroy every Christian, went to the High Priest in Jerusalem. He requested a letter addressed to synagogues in Damascus, requiring their cooperation in the persecution of any believers he found there, both men and women, so that he could bring them in chains to Jerusalem. As he was nearing Damascus on this mission, suddenly a brilliant light from heaven spotted down upon him! He fell to the ground and heard a voice saying to him 'Paul! Paul! Why are you persecuting me?' 'Who is speaking, sir?' Paul asked. And the voice replied, 'I am

Jesus, the one you are persecuting! Now get up and go into the city and await my further instructions.' The men with Paul stood speechless with surprise, for they heard the sound of someone's voice but saw no one! As Paul picked himself up off the ground, he found that he was blind. He had to be led into Damascus and was there three days, blind, going without food and water all that time." (Acts 9:1-9).

In Damascus the Lord directed a Christian believer to Paul. The believer addressed him, "Brother Paul, the Lord Jesus, who appeared to you on the road, has sent me so that you may be filled with the Holy Spirit and get your sight back. Instantly (it was as though scales fell from his eyes) Paul could see, and was immediately baptized. Paul began at once reversing his widespread reputation, from anti-Christian to pro-Christian, as a zealous Christian minister, evangelist, church organizer, Christian author, and Christlike miracle worker. One of his first widely reported miracles again dealt with blindness, but this time rather than his own it involved "a Jewish sorcerer, a false prophet named Bar-Jesus . . . . Paul, filled with the Holy Spirit, glared angrily at the sorcerer and said, 'You son of the devil, full of every sort of trickery and villainy, enemy of all that is good, will you never end your opposition to the Lord? And now God has laid his hand of punishment upon you, and you will be stricken awhile with blindness.' Instantly mist and darkness fell upon him, and he began wandering around begging for someone to take his hand and lead him . . . . ."

An increasing number of miracles began to accompany Paul's ministry, as it did with an increasing number of other disciples after Christ's Resurrection. Once Paul "came upon a man with crippled feet who had been that way from birth, so he never walked . . . . So Paul called to him, 'Stand up!' and the man leaped to his feet and started walking! . . . only a few days later, some Jews arrived from Antioch and Iconium and turned the crowds into a murderous mob that stoned Paul and dragged him out of the city, apparently dead. But as the believers stood around him, he got up and went back into the city!"

Persecutions of Paul and other disciples and ardent Christians seemed to increase as did the number and reputation of their miracles. Paul was imprisoned for years at a time and, on one occasion, while being transported as a prisoner on a ship,

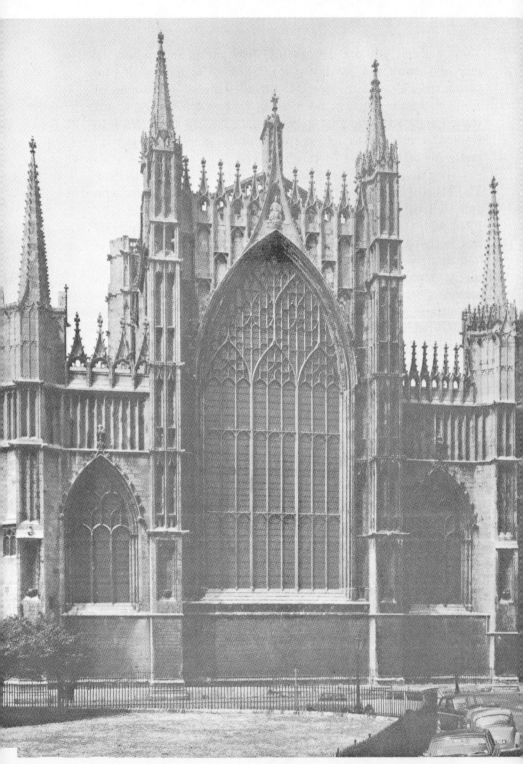

Paul The Apostle, after he saw the blinding light and heard the unseen voice, earned more credit than any other individual since Christ for the spread of Christian churches. In England these Christian cathedrals with their ornate towers owe a great debt to an apostle who wrote letters from prisons to small, informally organized church groups.

even predicted accurately that the ship would wreck and sink but that God safely would rescue all passengers onto an island. Though the persecution seemed to follow the same familiar pattern of orthodox Jews or other non-Christians pursuing the Christians, oftentimes capturing them, and then beating and imprisoning them, the miracles had wide-ranging character. There were miracles among believers as "when Paul laid his hands upon their heads, the Holy Spirit came on them, and they spoke in other languages and prophesied.... And God gave Paul the power to do unusual miracles, so that even when his handkerchief or parts of his clothing were placed upon sick people, they were healed, and any demons within them came out." (Acts 19:6-12).

The persecutors of the young Christians perhaps found their most exasperating dilemma in the matter of Christians in and out of jails. On more than one occasion the terms "in and out" were synonomous. An example occurred "when King Herod moved against some of the believers, and killed the apostle James (John's brother). When Herod saw how much this pleased the Jewish leaders, he arrested Peter during the Passover celebration and imprisoned him, placing him under the guard of sixteen soldiers. Herod's intention was to deliver Peter to the Jews for execution after the Passover. But earnest prayer was going up to God from the church for his safety all the time he was in prison.

"The night before he was to be executed, he was asleep, double-chained between two soldiers with others standing guard before the prison gate, when suddenly there was a light in the cell and an angel of the Lord stood beside Peter! The angel slapped him on the side to awaken him and said, 'Quick! Get up!' And the chains fell off his wrists! Then the angel told him, 'Get dressed and put on your shoes.' And he did. 'Now put on your coat and follow me!' the angel ordered.

"So Peter left the cell, following the angel. But all the time he thought it was a dream or vision, and didn't believe it was really happening. They passed the first and second cell blocks and came to the iron gate to the street, and this opened to them of its own accord! So they passed through and walked along together for a block, and then the angel left him.

"Peter finally realized what had happened! 'It's really

true!' he said to himself. 'The Lord has sent his angel and saved me from Herod and from what the Jews were hoping to do to me!'" (Acts 12:1-11).

Another occasion for the Christians—when stone walls did not a prison make nor iron bars a cage—concerned Paul. One day Paul and a few disciples "met a demon-possessed slave girl who was a fortune-teller, and earned much money for her masters." She followed behind them shouting, "'These men are servants of God and they have come to tell you how to have your sins forgiven.'

"This went on day after day until Paul, in great distress, turned and spoke to the demon within her. 'I command you in the name of Jesus Christ to come out of her,' he said. And instantly it left her.

"Her masters' hopes of wealth were now shattered; they grabbed Paul and Silas and dragged them before the judges at the marketplace.

"'These Jews are corrupting our city,' they shouted. 'They are teaching the people to do things that are against the Roman laws.'

"A mob was quickly formed against Paul and Silas, and the judges ordered them stripped and beaten with wooden whips. Again and again the rods slashed down across their bared backs: and afterwards they were thrown into prison. The jailer was threatened with death if they escaped, so he took no chances, but put them into the inner dungeon and clamped their feet into the stocks.

"Around midnight, as Paul and Silas were praying and singing hymns to the Lord—and the other prisoners were listening—suddenly there was a great earthquake; the prison was shaken to its foundations, all the doors flew open—and the chains of every prisoner fell off! The jailer wakened to see the prison doors wide open, and assuming the prisoners had escaped, he drew his sword to kill himself.

"But Paul yelled to him, 'Don't do it! We are all here!'" (Acts 16:16-28).

Paul the Apostle continued his ministry to an indeterminate date when as far as is known he died a natural death. His fame continues increasing to this day, and in addition to all his other work his many letters to Christians at farflung churches

he organized form many of the most historic chapters of the
New Testament. Throughout the ages Christians have considered the Apostle Paul the New Testament's most towering
personality next to Christ Jesus.

Born At Age 60

Before birth the sage spent 60 years inside his mother, was born with hair already white, and at birth spoke at once to the plum tree under which he was born. Small wonder that at birth he was greeted with the name Old Master. Traditionally Old Master's name was associated with authorship of the longest-lasting book of influence ever produced in China, the *Tao Te Ching*, or the *Way and its Power*. This classic Chinese master-piece has 88 brief chapters, a sacred number in China. Tao (pronounced dow) is the pathway or doorway through which the 10,000 creatures of earth have come. Stressing nonviolence in a country where warring states fought often, *Tao Te Ching* more than any other significant Chinese book condemned warfare. According to the Tao, warfare brings only devastation and decay, and even to enjoy weapons means to enjoy slaughter and brings only distress instead of peace.

Later Taoism emphasized magic and magicians, developing a priesthood that in turn resulted in many temples. These practitioners made many claims regarding such things as transforming or dissolving old bodies into young ones and calling up ghosts as needed. The faithful followed a Celestial Master, the latest being the sixty-third.

The Taoists organized various open and secret societies, many of them a problem for the Communists in later years in China. In 1957 the Chinese government sponsored the Chinese Taoist Association in an attempt to unify the Taoists in "support for socialist construction."

The Taoist philosophy of naturalness and tranquility continues to have a great influence in China, much as water gently overcoming rough obstacles. The Taoist principle of learning landscapes or other subjects so thoroughly that the artist gets inside and participates continues to greatly influence Chinese literature and painting. Taoism, and to a lesser extent Buddhism and Confucianism, continues to represent the soul of China.

From Confucious (551-479 B.C.) came less a supernatural religious emphasis, at least compared to Taoism and Buddhism, than traditional respect for authority and the veneration of superior powers including the veneration of ancestors. Part of this was in consideration of the large family unit in China. Master K'ung, K'ung-Fu-tse, or Confucious as the incoming Jesuit missionaries later called him, made many wise pronouncements concerning sometimes religious but more often political and social subjects. One interesting Confucious axiom was a negative

This family temple, or ancestral hall, personifies in China the established and the aged. Within these walls it was easy to understand why Lao Tse was born at age 60 or why Confucius was so popular in his veneration of authority and ancestors.

of the Golden Rule: "What I do not wish others to do to me, that also I wish not to do to them." Confucianism together with Taoism and Buddhism before the birth of Christ began shaping China. China's *Tao Te Ching*, its *Way and its Power*, points back traditionally to the Old Master, born with white hair at age 60 after which he lived 160 years, epitomizing the veneration heritage in Chinese history. (For an interesting volume reflecting painstaking research into the history of world religions read *The Faiths of Mankind* by Geoffrey Parrinder, Thomas Y. Crowell Company, 1965.)

Born 547 Times

GAUTAMA BUDDHA (circa 563-483 B.C.). India. Hill country near Nepal.

The last of his human births was into the ruling warrior caste of Hindus to the Gautama (or Gatama) family. His father Suddhodana and his mother Maya (or Maya Devi) named the newborn son Siddhartha (or Siddhattha). At his birth his mother had a dream of a white elephant entering her side, and this was interpreted as a son who would be a Buddha, "an enlightened one." At birth he cried out in a voice of a lion, "I am the chief in the world, this is my last birth, there is now no existence again."

After rearing the youth in luxury, the family married him to an unusually beautiful princess named Yashodara. Because seers warned King Suddhodana that Prince Siddhartha would renounce the world when he saw certain signs, the king confined the prince and princess to the palace and gardens. However, by age 29 the prince had gotten outside the gardens, and these four signs appeared to him: an elderly man, a sick man, a corpse, and an ascetic. They reminded him of sorrow in the world, life's brevity, and renunciation from the world. Thus began the Buddhist religion's great concern with suffering.

Gautama, the family name by which Prince Siddhartha commonly became known, grew so unhappy and restless he decided upon a Great Renunciation. Gautama arose at night, left behind him his sleeping wife and a son named Rahula by now born to them, and with a faithful charioteer and horse galloped

30 leagues from home. There Gautama dispatched his companions homeward, shaved off his hair, and procuring a plain robe began living the life of an ascetic.

For a number of years Gautama strove to find spiritual answers from religious experts, but after subscribing to the teachings of a Yoga expert he discovered nothingness rather than peace. Subsequently he tried fasting and other methods of severe mortification till his ribs protruded like an old hut's rafters, the skin of his stomach touched his spine, and his head skin clung to his skull. So extreme were such severities, five other ascetics stayed with Gautama in awe, and even today a number of outstanding statues depict his stage of emaciation. After some time he found no value in self-torture and resumed eating, and with this the disgusted ascetics departed his company.

But Gautama continued his search until he arrived in Gaya, beside a tributary of the Ganges, and continuing a few miles past the town he seated himself under a tree. This was the Bo-tree, or Bodhi-tree, of great fame, the sacred fig tree or "tree of enlightenment." All Buddhas throughout the ages have been enlightened at this tree, otherwise known as the Diamond Seat. Gautama resolved that until he had obtained spiritual enlightenment, here he would stay. After a day and night of meditating, understanding came to him. Here he obtained all knowledge, including the fact that he had been born 547 times, including previous existences as bird, animal, and man. Thus he became a Buddha, truly "an enlightened one," and attained Nirvana, the end of desire and thus the cessation of reincarnation.

The Buddha departed the tree for the great religious center Benares and en route met the five ascetics who earlier had deserted him. Though at first they chose to ignore him, his radiance convinced them, and they accompanied him as his first converts. The group proceeded to a deer park four miles north of Benares, and there the Buddha preached his first sermon. Many followers became monks, leading to the establishment of numerous Buddhist monasteries. Gautama's son Rahula joined him and became a monk. The Buddha disregarded all caste discrimination including such against women and permitted the founding of a female order in which his wife Yashodara became a nun. He taught his followers to beg for their food and even returned to the door of his father's palace and stood begging.

The Buddha continued to preach and teach for 40 years. Then one day a metal-worker named Chunda fed him some tainted pork, and Gautama was seized with violent pains and forbade anyone else to touch it. Dysentery developed and in a grove surrounded by weeping disciples the Buddha uttered his final words: "All composite things are doomed to extinction. Exert yourselves in wakefulness." Thus the Buddha died at about 80 years of age (circa 483 B.C.). As followed Hindu custom his friends cremated the Buddha's body, though some of the remains were distributed as relics to seven cities. For example, a tooth and collar bone went to Ceylon and hairs to Burma.

Buddhism has been a missionary religion, unrestricted by caste or sex, and since Buddha's death has continued to prosper, often alongside the other great missionary religions of Hinduism, Islam, and Christianity. Buddhism teaches a Middle Way, between the extremes of asceticism and sensuality. A great impetus to the Buddhist movement came from the Indian king Ashoka, who ascended to the Indian throne about 272 B.C. Apparently Ashoka converted to Buddhism, and some say he became a monk even though he continued to rule. Frequently he visited sacred Buddhist places and relics there enshrined. In A.D. 1898, roughly 2,000 years after Ashoka, one such sacred place became a site near Kushinara in India, where a casket was found with an inscription reading, "this deposit of relics is of the blessed Buddha of the Shakyas." Millions of faithful Buddhists throughout Southeast Asia found added impetus to recite the daily threefold Refuge Formula:

"I go to the Buddha for refuge,
I go to the Dhamma (doctrine) for refuge,
I go to the Sangha (monastic order) for refuge."

This temple in Tokyo, Japan, is part of a religious tradition that includes Buddha's 547th birth that occurred about 500 years before Christ.

At left is seated Buddha, dating back to about the third century A.D., and at right, dating back to about the same era, is a spiritual image of Buddhism known as a bodhisattva.

Changing A Government By Means Of Soul Force

MAHATMA GANDHI (A.D. October 2, 1869-January 30, 1948). India. Parbandar.

Known as "the white city" because of a white bridge that led inland from a site all but surrounded by water, Porbandar on the Kathiawar peninsula on the coast of India was the birthplace of Mohandas Karamchand Gandhi, in recent times India's most revered personality. He was the third son of Karamchand Gandhi, prime minister of the area. The birth occurred in a massive three-story home which had belonged to the Gandhi family for five generations and which, though greatly altered, stands today.

The youth matured in a family devoted to the god Krishna, the enchanting blue-faced god who was counted among the 12 incarnations of the great Vishnu, one of the three supreme Hindu gods. As the youngest of four children Mohandas was pampered by the family but was closest to his religiously devout mother, considered by him "the center of his life." As the son of the local prime minister, he was treated like a young prince not only in his own household but by the area residents.

Befitting his privileged role in life Mohandas studied law in London and upon his return to India became an advocate of the Bombay High Court. In 1893 he inaugurated a policy of passive resistance in South Africa in protest against the inhumane conditions imposed upon his Indian people there. He preached a message of nonviolence through soul force, a message that he carried from South Africa against the British government in India.

At right 17-year-old Mahatma Gandhi sits beside his brother Laxmidas.

Despite his family background of devotion to the god Krishna, he became a student of religions in addition to Hindu and Jain, was greatly influenced by the doctrine and methods of Christ, and gave considerable credit to the writings of Tolstoy. Christ's "Sermon On The Mount" had special influence on Mohandas' developing concept of nonviolence. His bestowal of wealth upon the poor, his life of asceticism, and his religious fervor won for him the surname of Mahatma (Great Soul).

Mahatma Gandhi not only struggled successfully for Indian independence, he greatly improved the lot and outlook of outcasts. It is to his credit that caste discrimination is no longer legal in India. Gandhi's stature became such that many people in India and elsewhere in the world came to regard him as an incarnation of God on earth, an avatar.

Gandhi was assassinated by a Hindu Mahasabha fanatic in 1948. It is ironic that Gandhi's assassination came about because of a conflict in interpretation of the great Hindu epic "Bhagavad Gita." Gandhi's assassin, Nathuram Godse, believed that in the "Bhagavad Gita" the god Krishna had ordered the warrior Arjuna to go into battle and take human lives. But Mahatma Gandhi insisted that Krishna had meant for the battle to take place only in the human heart.

The renaming of Mohandas as Great Soul proved entirely appropriate. No other leader of the 20th century has so shown that world events can be altered through the concentrated force of mankind's supernatural powers. Social including racial reformers in America and throughout the world have proved amazingly successful with the concentrated force of these powers. The will of people to change national events by the miraculous power of a "nation's mind" over world matter is more and more obvious.

Today every community of size, as well as many villages throughout India, features a bust of Mahatma Gandhi which the faithful continually garland with marigold flowers. The full impact of Gandhi's nonviolent soul force is yet to be felt in this changing modern world. (A massive and meticulously detailed account of Gandhi's life and death can be found in *The Life And Death Of Mahatma Gandhi,* Robert Payne, E. P. Dutton & Co., 1969.)

Mahatma Gandhi as millions of his followers remember him.

Circling Nature's Laws

URI GELLER (A.D. December 20, 1946-   ). Israel. Tel Aviv.

Itzhak and Margaret Geller were Jewish refugees from Hungary, where his father was a rabbi and where her relatives were in business and could claim distant relationship with Sigmund Freud. To support his family including their son Uri, the hard-pressed father held an assortment of jobs, including lollipop salesman, cab driver, and soldier. Young Uri's mother worked as a seamstress to supplement family income, until times improved and she took in roomers at a small hotel. Uri always admired his father, who, as a handsome soldier, seemed as attracted to dangerous fighting as dangerous women were attracted to him; but Uri seemed to grow even closer to his mother. From early years he saw his parents' marriage disintegrating, separation leading to eventual divorce.

Uri's first amazing experience occurred at age three or four. He was playing in the shadowy overgrown yard of a large abandoned grey house across from his home in Tel Aviv. Suddenly the rustling of the trees stopped, and there was a loud, high-pitched ringing in his ears. Then a brilliant, silvery mass of light came between him and the sun, moving nearer until it was close overhead. A sharp pain hit Uri's forehead, making him feel as if knocked backwards, and then he lost consciousness. Sometime later—he was never sure how long—he woke and rushed home and told his mother. While he realized that something important had happened, a child so young, of course, could not convince his mother of such a tale. And though he returned to the shadowy yard many times after that, hoping to see the brilliant, silver mass of light again, it never reappeared.

After the shadowy-yard experience, Uri startled his mother in a different way. On various occasions he would tell her with detailed accuracy what she had done while they were apart, or, on other occasions, would voice her words before she could utter them.

When Uri was about six his father bought him a watch, which the bored student took to school with eagerness. At school he would glance at the watch many times, anticipating the bell ringing for recess. He began discovering with amazement that as he eagerly looked, his watch would jump a half hour or so ahead of the school clock, causing him to have to set his watch back. Compounding Uri's surprise, the minute hand sometimes would spin four or five hours or more ahead. He left the watch home for his mother to check, but at home the watch continued to keep accurate, normal time for weeks. So he took the watch with him again to school, and this time in order to keep it in better view he took it off his wrist and set it in front of him. His thoughts wandered for a while and then he glanced down and saw the hands spinning around as if the watch had gone wild. He shouted for the teacher to look at the watch and held it up for all to see. As everybody laughed at him he became very embarrassed and realized for the first time that he had to be careful about what he said away from home. When he told his mother what happened, she listened carefully before promising to get him another one when she could. He never wore the old one again.

Boasting another new watch at last, he took it to school and an even stranger event happened. After keeping good time for a number of days, the watch hands caught his attention one day by seeming to twist upward against the crystal until bent. This time of course he told no one at school, but when he arrived home he found his father there on an infrequent visit and told both parents. They looked at him with open doubts, and Uri never received another watch during his childhood.

But though unusual and without close friends at school he did have companions, and one day during lunch a classmate, who was wearing a watch, exclaimed that his watch had just moved an hour ahead. When Uri asked to hold the watch his companion agreed, and each time Uri would order the watch two or three times to "Move" the watch would race ahead again. Convinced at last that he was an outstanding magician, the class began complimenting Uri instead of laughing. Shortly, at age eight or nine, he was at home eating soup only to have the bowl of his spoon bend down, spill hot soup into his lap, and then separate and fall from the handle of the spoon. Uri estimates that even in childhood such strange things as this occurred 30 or 40 times a year. Sometimes he would accompany his mother and some of her friends to a coffee shop, and there the spoons on the coffee shop table would curl up out of shape. The harassed waiters would hurry to remove the abnormal cutlery, lest the shop be accused of providing inferior utensils. His mother warned him in private that she hoped she did not have to take him to a doctor. During another of his father's more and more infrequent visits home, his parents discussed taking him to a psychiatrist, then decided to wait hoping that he would outgrow this phase. When they at last felt they had enough and told him he must go to a psychiatrist, he angrily refused, telling them that with their marriage breaking up they were the ones who needed a psychiatrist, not their nine-year-old son. Instead of going to a psychiatrist, Uri tried for a while to concentrate like other boys upon sports such as basketball and soccer.

Though no longer unexpected, it still was something of a traumatic experience when his father and mother divorced. But Uri's unusual experiences continued in and out of his mother's home. Once, when visiting a zoo, he convinced his mother to leave with him at once, and just as they cleared the zoo area the gates closed behind them because a tiger had broken loose as people fled for their lives. On another occasion he discovered a locked combination lock at home, and not knowing the combination he unlocked it by concentrating his mind upon it for two minutes.

Even school grew more exciting. While yet in his preteens Uri found that it was easier, and certainly more fun, to concentrate more upon the minds of the brightest students than to concentrate upon textbooks. During examinations he would concentrate upon the brightest student and write that student's answers upon his own paper. Receiving excellent papers in iden-

Uri Geller.

tical pairs the teachers began to suspect copying. Eventually they placed Uri alone at a desk in a far corner of the room. However, all this proved was that Uri did not need to look at the bright student in order to read the student's mind. Uri also read teachers' minds or performed unusual demonstrations for them. Uri explained to one teacher what she had done in her absence. Another woman teacher brought four very old broken watches to class. After Uri passed his hand over each watch, the watch began working. No wonder the former laughing stock at school became known instead for his brilliant mind and amazing feats.

Though a sensitive and at times lonely child, Uri displayed more courage and was more adventuresome than many youths, for example, scuba diving in shark-infested waters and losing himself during lonely explorations in dark caves. A handsome male like his father, Uri soon found that girls were attracted to him and he to them. His sexual experiences while yet a teenager and unmarried would not have pleased his grandfather, the rabbi. But beginning at age 18, Uri's bravery pleased his father. His courageous adventurism overcoming his instinctive apprehension about parachuting, Uri enlisted as a paratrooper, and his amazing experiences continued through the historic Six-Day War of 1967. At the start of the Six-Day War, Uri and some other soldiers were rushed toward a place called Ramala, several miles from Jerusalem. Uri had a premonition that he would be hurt or wounded rather than killed, but when he looked a friend of his in the eyes he saw that the friend would die in the upcoming battle. Uri asked his friend to shake hands, and though his friend asked him "Why," they shook hands and then Uri walked away. Uri prayed to God, asking God if there was any way to save his friend's life or to keep himself from being hurt or wounded. Uri could not sleep that night before the group went into action, as he sought answers that never came.

In the battle the next day Jordanian fire indeed killed Uri's friend as much hand-to-hand fighting took place near a cemetery wall. Uri had eight men under his command. Though shot in the left hand Uri ordered some of his men to accompany him up a hill and try to take a pillbox whose fire was pinning them down. As Uri led two men up the hill an Arab jumped from behind a nearby rock, and from easy range shot twice at Uri and missed. The incredulous Uri then got his own gun just as high as his waist, shot from his waist, and killed the Arab. Soon after this there was a blast, and as something hit Uri's right arm and something else his forehead near his eyes, he blacked out. He thought he was dead, but instead awoke in a hospital with arms and head bandaged. For what it was worth, his premonitions had proved correct.

During three months of convalescing, though still partly bandaged, he was asked to work with groups of children, sometimes several hundred strong, in postwar Israel. And though telepathy was not officially part of the curriculum, before long he found himself holding their attention by once more displaying his powers. For the first time the learning process became a two-way street as a youngster in one of the groups displayed powers almost as amazing as Uri's own. The youngster brought some keys from home, and as he and Uri sat together the keys, with just the slightest touch, bent 90 degrees within half a minute. With some other youngster seated near Uri the bend would be only 10 to 45 degrees. Together Uri and the gifted youngster could bend nails or move watches with only the slightest touch, or read each other's minds in terms of identifying cards or drawings the other had made in supposed secret.

Uri reached age 21 and worldwide fame at about the same time. Discharged from the Israeli army late in 1968, he began responding to requests to demonstrate his powers to increasingly large audiences. His demonstrations proved effective about 75 percent to 80 percent of the time, there seeming to be some corollary between Uri's overall success and the makeup of his audience. Among those hearing of Uri was an American medical doctor and scientist, Dr. Andrija Puharich, who came to Israel in August 1971 to head a group interested in a closer scientific look at this reported phenomenon. Uri acceded to the scientist's request to go under hypnosis and have his responses recorded on a tape recorder. The only problem was, though a number of scientists and onlookers simultaneously heard Uri's response under hypnosis in several hour-long sessions, the words on tape sooner or later, and usually sooner, would self-destruct. At the end of the first hypnosis session Uri asked to hear the playback of what he had said under hypnosis. He listened to his words taped during hypnosis, describing his childhood, going back to age three and the shadowy garden when the bright light appeared. Then abruptly the tone of Uri's taped voice changed to a strange sound, and Uri—seized with agitation—grabbed the tape recorder, stopped it, ejected the tape, and the tape dematerialized before everyone's eyes. It vanished from Uri's hands as if it had not been there in the first place. Still agitated,he rushed outside the room and was in a building elevator when found. But the tape itself never was found.

The scientific group discovered that recording Uri on tape was an impossible task. The tape recording equipment simply became as abnormal as keys or watches exposed to Uri's energy. The recording equipment involved in his hypnosis sessions would start or stop without being activated by human control. The recording tapes themselves would either dematerialize inside the recorder, would play out blank, or if by some capricious whim they did in fact play out with words they then would dematerialize. As taping sessions continued, the computerlike voice that replaced Uri's on tapes that would play identified itself as from a spacecraft named "Spectra." Various well-respected witnesses in the scientific group investigating Uri went on record witnessing that the voice said it was from a planet thousands of light years away and that one of its purposes was to help Uri bring peace to earth. The voice advised taking a camera to a specified place near Tel Aviv, and Uri and an investigator rushed to the spot. There in the presence of several witnesses Uri photographed a bright oval UFO. It was one of a number of occasions when Uri would photograph UFOs in various parts of the world, and millions of copies of his photographs would be reproduced in periodicals and books. On another occasion Uri felt the urge to go to another place near Tel Aviv. He asked his friends to wait behind as he approached a bluish-white pulsating light, a UFO that Uri heard as crackling with electronic energy, sounding to him like the chirping of many crickets. Uri entered a trancelike state and was sucked up into something that seemed to have panels. A shape that was dark and indistinguishable put in his hand a ballpoint refill cartridge with the same serial number as a similar cartridge that had earlier dematerialized in the presence of Uri and others during a demonstration scene.

Uri's fame brought him prompt invitations from many nations. In the spring of 1972 he accepted an invitation to give demonstrations in various parts of Germany. In Germany reporters asked him to concentrate on stopping the forward progress of a powerful cable car, which he stopped, and later asked him to concentrate on stopping a moving escalator, which he did also. On a subsequent jet flight between Germany and England, Uri's camera rose without visible assistance from under his seat, stopped in mid-air in front of him, and though Uri saw nothing outside his airplane window he took some shots on impulse. When the negatives printed they would show a clearly identified UFO.

Stanford Research Institute in America expressed interest in testing Uri. He made a brief preliminary visit in August of 1972, helping to complete arrangements for future SRI testing. A number of scientific-minded American celebrities, including Astronaut Edgar Mitchell, met him during this trip. Interspersed with several informal tests of Uri in America were the continuation of the phenomena with the tape recorder plus a large amount of levitation phenomena as a vase would float in from one room to another or an ash tray or other object would leap off a table. All objects, instead of breaking, would land with a faint clinking sound on a table, floor, or other available landing area.

Uri left America for three months and then returned in November of 1972 with arrangements completed for testing at Stanford Research Institute. Almost at once it became clear that Uri's second visit to America was no more that of your everyday tourist's than had been his first. Uri initially was a guest of Dr. Puharich whose home was in Ossining, an hour or so drive from the New York airport where Uri landed. Uri was greeted by the sight of the doctor's dog, lying on the floor, trembling noticeably. That is, the dog was lying there one instant, and the next instant the dog had dematerialized. Within seconds the dog reappeared far down the highway coming toward the house, the dog's appearance still that of agitation. This event was a preamble. After passing the SRI tests with flying colors, successfully identifying hidden objects against 1,000,000 to 1 odds, for example, and after successful television demonstrations on American shows such as the Jack Paar, Merv Griffin, and "CBS 60 Minutes," the famous Uri returned to the New

York City area. He had gone shopping for a present for a girl-friend and was jogging home to his apartment when all at once he had the feeling of running backwards for a couple of steps, and then of being sucked upward, his eyes seeming to close momentarily. With returning vision he saw himself flying through the air toward Dr. Puharich's house in Ossining, at least an hour's normal drive distant from where Uri had been launched off the streets of New York a seeming moment earlier. Uri next found himself flying into and through Dr. Puharich's porch screen, then crashing onto a glass-top table, knocking the table over, and breaking the table's glass. Except for feeling cold and quite thirsty, and at first afraid to move, Uri's wingless flight off New York streets in the blinking of an eye had caused him no harm.

However strange Uri's experiences to date, his most portentous, widely tested demonstrations were ahead. Following his second spectacular American trip, the British Broadcasting Corporation invited Uri to London in November 1973. There on BBC radio and later on BBC television Uri invited those tuned in to concentrate upon their own keys, spoons, forks, or nails and see what would happen. Calls came in from all over the British Isles reporting the bending of those items or the proving out of one of several telepathic feats demonstrated over the air by Uri. Uri was invited to perform over the air in Germany, Switzerland, Norway, Sweden, and Denmark, where similar experiences occurred. A strange side effect was mysterious malfunctioning of major mechanical or electrical equipment at or near or some distance from broadcasting equipment used during or after Uri was on the air. In addition, leading newspapers requested to be involved in his demonstrations. Representatives from newspapers asked Uri to concentrate at the same predetermined time that the paper's readers would be asked to concentrate. Even though Uri was across the channel in Paris for one such coordination, back in London a paper reported from England's side of the channel this final tabulation from its readers: 1,031 clocks and watches restarted; 293 forks and spoons bent or broken; 51 other objects bent or broken. Total items reported affected: 1,375. In Denmark 1,098 readers of a Danish magazine phoned in miraculous experiences. Instead of concentrating upon her broken watches one elderly lady reported concentrating upon her arthritic knee, and it was healed.

Uri says that someday he hopes that healing will play a significant role in the miraculous results of his so-called "Geller Effect." Though claiming no organized religious allegiance or mode of worship he has stated strong belief in God. The powerful energies that work through him, sometimes capriciously it would seem, he credits to unseen energy origins between this earth and God. He is seeking the same answers as those who test him. Both he and many of them believe that some day his strange energies not only will be understood but will work to the great benefit of all mankind. (For a book that indeed should prove to the reader that truth is stranger than fiction read Uri's fascinating autobiography, *Uri Geller: My Story*, Praeger, 1975. For a valuable work documented in detail read *Uri*, Henry K. Puharich, Doubleday, 1974.)

Forming A Woman Out Of A Man's Rib

GOD (   ).

The God of Judaism and Christianity is a God who always has been and always will be. For both religions God is explained in the holy book, the Bible. The first sentence of the Bible, Genesis 1:1, starts with perhaps the most widely printed four words in the world, "In the beginning God . . . ." As God revealed himself to the prophets and other selected people, to the Jews followed by the Christians, they wrote down their revelations in a written record called the Bible. It was transcribed over a period of about a thousand years, starting about 800 B.C. The Jewish Bible, called by them the Holy Scriptures but better known as the Old Testament, originally was written in Hebrew. In the Old Testament writings the Jews anticipated the coming of a Messiah, or savior. In the New Testament, originally written in Greek, the record shows that the Jews rejected Jesus Christ as a hoped-for Messiah deliverer, but Christians insisted that Jesus truly was the Messiah long-awaited.

Before the invention of moveable type in the fifteenth century the Bible did not appear in any form except handwritten copies. This means that the Bible was copied by hand for approximately 1200 years after the original Bible was completed about A.D. 200. Such handwritten copies were called manuscripts, from the Latin words *manu* meaning "by hand" and *scriptum* meaning "written." Most ancient manuscripts were written on either papyrus (bullrush plants beaten into sheet form) or parchments (treated animal skin). Writing typically was accomplished with a reed cut into the shape of a writing pen using ink made of soot, gum, and water. Writing was mainly a job for trained and skilled men. Some, like the Apostle Paul who wrote so many widely read chapters in the New Testament, dictated writings to a secretary called a scribe and then signed the result in their own handwriting to support authenticity.

The Bible begins not only with a description of God, but also with a description of creation. In the beginning God created the heavens and the earth (Genesis 1:1). The Bible does not explain how long ago creation began but states that the "earth was without form, and void, and darkness was upon the face of the deep. And the spirit of God moved upon the face of the waters" (Genesis 1:2). Then God said, "Let there be light," and so light shone upon the universe. God then divided darkness and light into night and day. On the second day God separated vapors to form the sky above and the oceans below. On the third day God separated dry land and water. On the fourth day God created the sun and the moon and the stars, on the fifth day birds and fish, and on the sixth added animals and man. On the seventh day God rested.

The second chapter of Genesis explains in more detail the creation of man. The Hebrew word Eden means "delight," and an exciting garden created by God fitted the description "Garden of Delight." Watered by four rivers, it was luxuriant with flowers, trees, and fruit. In the center of the garden stood a strange tree called the Tree of Life. A second noteworthy tree, called the Tree of Knowledge of Good and Evil, stood also in the garden. After forming man from the dust of the ground God breathed into man's nostrils the breath of life, and he became a living soul. God then took the man and put him in the Garden of Eden as its gardener, to tend and care for it. But the Lord God gave the man this warning: "You may eat any fruit from the garden except fruit from the Tree of Knowledge of Good and Evil. The day you eat from it you shall surely die."

From this time forward the Bible calls man "Adam," a name that means "man." God decided that Adam needed a companion to offset Adam's loneliness. As soon as Adam had called all the birds and animals to him and given them names, God put Adam into a deep sleep. As Adam slumbered, from his

47

side God took a rib and closed up the flesh. From this rib God made a woman, named Eve, and gave her to Adam as his wife. "This is it!" Adam exclaimed. "She is part of my own bone and flesh. Her name is 'woman' because she was taken out of a man."

Although both Adam and Eve were naked, neither of them was embarrassed nor ashamed. They enjoyed their assignment of keeping the garden beautiful. Sometimes God walked in the garden and talked with them. But one day a serpent came to Eve and tempted her to eat fruit from the Tree of Knowledge of Good and Evil. The serpent explained that God had lied about what would happen if she ate the tree's fruit. "You'll not die," the serpent hissed. "God knows very well that the instant you eat it you will become like him, for your eyes will be opened— you will be able to distinguish good from evil!" The woman was convinced. How lovely and fresh looking it was. And it would make her so wise. So she ate some of the fruit and gave some to her husband, and he ate it too. And as they ate it, suddenly they became aware of their nakedness, and were embarrassed. So they strung fig leaves together to cover themselves around the hips.

That evening they heard the sound of the Lord God walking in the garden, and they hid themselves among the trees. God demanded of Adam, "Why are you hiding?" Adam replied, "I heard you coming and didn't want you to see me naked. So I hid." At this God asked, "Who told you you were naked? Have you eaten fruit from the tree I warned you about?" "Yes," Adam admitted, "but it was the woman you gave me who brought me some, and I ate it." Then God demanded of the woman, "How could you do such a thing?" Her only reply was, "The serpent tricked me." Adam and Eve had made their choice. God drove them from the garden where everything had been given them so freely. Outside in the cruel world they must work and suffer to attain their goals. As God expelled them from the garden, he placed mighty angels at the east of this garden of Eden with a flaming sword to guard the entrance to the Tree of Life. (Worthwhile volumes for further reading include *The Living Bible*, Tyndale House Publishers, 1973, and the three-volume *Christian Book of Knowledge* compiled by Processing And Books, Inc., 1969).

Over the centuries believers have built millions of places of worship, so much so it is difficult to imagine what a countryside would resemble with none. For centuries St. Mark's in Venice, as shown here, has been one of the most elaborate cathedrals.

Forming Many Mouths, Eyes, And Faces On One's Own Body

LORD KRISHNA (circa 3000 B.C.). India.

After reincarnations during billions of years in the past, the supreme deity became reincarnated in the historical personage of Lord Krishna about 5,000 years ago in India. When Krishna was merely a small baby the gigantic demoness Putana attempted to kill him, but instead he sucked her breast and pulled out her life. This obvious miracle power in infancy is the difference between a real God and a God manufactured in someone's imagination.

The account of Krishna's activities is in the famed "Bhagavad Gita" or "Song of the Blessed Lord," one of the classics of religious literature. The "Bhagavad Gita" has greatly influenced Hinduism for more than a thousand years. This poem occurs in its present form as an episode in the enormous epic, the *Mahabharata,* which consists of stories of heroes, gods, and godlings of the classic days. The *Mahabharata* was compiled during a period of 800 years (400 B.C. to A.D. 400), and its 100,000 couplets deal primarily with the exploits of Kshatriya clans, in particular with the fall of the Kuru (Kaurava) princes at the hands of their relatives, the Pandavas, guided by the hero-god Krishna. The "Bhagavad Gita" was interwoven into the *Mahabharata* about the first century A.D. A poem widely acclaimed as remarkable in many ways, its devotional and intellectual power has won more converts to Hinduism than any other single Hindu work.

50

About 3,500 years after the supreme deity became reincarnated in the historical personage of Lord Krishna, followers of Hinduism built this Bodh Gaya temple in India, one of numerous Hindu temples used by Lord Krishna faithful.

The "Bhagavad Gita" tells the story of Arjuna, a great warrior of the family of Pandavas, who voiced misgivings about leading his brothers and their allies into battle against the Kuru princes. These princes were sons of Arjuna's blind uncle, Dhritirashtra, and thus Arjuna's own close relatives. Arjuna's charioteer was the hero-god Krishna, who stood poised at his side ready for instant battle. Krishna reassured Arjuna that it was all right to drive the chariot into battle with its milk-white steeds between the battle lines. For one thing, Arjuna was not attacking the souls of his enemy-relatives, because the real self, the spirit, of each one was indestructible. For another thing, Arjuna's duty was to follow the orders of God, regardless of how humanly illogical such orders might seem on the surface.

To prove to Arjuna that he indeed was Brahma, the one eternal God who has assumed human form, Krishna transformed himself into Vishnu, the eternal Brahman in god-form, displaying to the astounded Arjuna his true self, endowed with numberless mouths, countless eyes, and faces turned in every direction, his entity clothed with ornaments, wreaths, and divine apparel scented with heavenly fragrance. At this sight Arjuna's every hair bristled with awe, and his voice gave way to adoration. He prayed that the overly sublime vision be removed and that the god return to the accustomed disguise of Krishna, the charioteer. The god acceded to this request, and accompanied by the now-convinced Arjuna proceeded to overcome the enemy.

For 2,000 years, since assimilation of the "Bhagavad Gita" into the *Mahabharata* in the first century A.D., one of the most important aspects of Hinduism has been Bhakti, ardent and hopeful devotion to a particular diety. This account of Krishna and his warrior, Arjuna, has helped shape the religious practices of hundreds of millions of people over the centuries. (A clearly written and well-organized approach to the study of world religions can be found in *How The Great Religions Began*, Joseph Gaer, Dodd, Mead & Company, 1966.)

Helping Mentally Unbalanced People By Sitting Next To Them

MEHER BABA (A.D. 1894-January 31, 1969). India.
Poona.

He was born to middle-class parents who named him Merwan Sheriaji Irani. Riding a bicycle home from college one day
in 1913 he espied an old woman seated under a tree. Their
glances met, she beckoned to him, and he parked his bicycle
and walked to her. They spoke no word to each other, but he
learned later that the old woman was the Muslim saint Hazrat
Babajan, reportedly more than a hundred years old at this time.
Instead of them speaking, the old woman rose and embraced
him, and after the two spent a while in silence he left. This was
the first of a number of meetings between them, as he continued to stop from time to time and sit beside her in silence.

It was during one such visit, early in 1914, that she kissed
him on the forehead, and soon after his return home he fell into
a trance. Though his eyes were open he saw nothing for three
days, and even after three days when he began to move about
he moved mechanically, unconscious of his surroundings. For
the next nine months he failed to respond to medical treatment.
Then he was taken to certain Indian spiritual leaders for help
and eventually to Sai Baba of Shirdi, before whom he pros-
trated himself. When Merwan arose, Sai Baba addressed him as
God-Almighty-Sustainer. Merwan then was sent to Upasani Maharaj, who, under Sai Baba's spiritual guidance, was at the time
naked and fasting. When Upasani Maharaj saw Merwan on this
first occasion, he threw a stone at him that hit him on the fore-

The same Hindu ardor that inspired these ornate temples and temple decorations in India inspired Meher Baba to go to cemeteries, garbage dumps, and latrines to seek the afflicted.

head. The reason was to bring him back to consciousness.

Near the end of 1921 Upasani returned Merwan completely to normal consciousness, and addressing him as "God incarnated as man" told him that he saluted him. Disciples were drawn now to Merwan, and they gave him the name of Meher Baba, or Compassionate Father.

In 1925 Meher Baba stopped speaking, a silence he continued until death 44 years later. It was during a ten-year-span in this life of speechlessness that Meher Baba did something different from other leaders. He and four or five devotees began to comb India's countryside, seeking out many of the mentally unbalanced traditionally at large in that country. He sought a particular class of these unbalanced whom he called masts, or God-intoxicated souls. They had renounced the world and often were partly or completely naked, their bodies covered with filth. Though many lived in cemeteries, garbage dumps, or latrines, wherever they could be found, Baba went to them. He would sit beside them for a while in silence and then proceed to the next.

Such silent communication between Baba and the masts often worked thereapeutic miracles. His silent presence spoke much louder than words as he exhibited a tranquilizing effect immeasureable in human terms.

Today Meher Baba has many worshipers in the West as well as East. His oftentimes unusual actions, including his self-imposed silence from 1925 to the day of his death on January 31, 1969, did not deter his many followers. They have felt that such mysterious actions were yet another example that God often works in mysterious ways. (For an account of Eastern metaphysical leaders, authored by a qualified observer who spent many years in India, see *Gurus, Swamis, And Avataras*. Henry Harper, The Westminister Press, 1972.)

Making Invisible Oneself And Friends

SRI UPASANI BABA MAHARAJ (A.D. May 5, 1870-December 24, 1941). India. Satana in the state of Maharashtra.

The child Kasahinath Govind Upasani Sastri, later to become known as Sri Upasani Baba Maharaj, was born into a Brahmin family that served as priests to the community. At school Kasahinath developed a dislike for his teacher, and so his family permitted him to drop out of school and receive improvised instruction at home.

In accordance with traditional teaching that a person's body is the prison of a person's real self, he began to describe his body as an enemy and remark, "It fattens upon our labors and forces us to endure the drudgery and pain of education and the pursuit of a calling for its sake." Consequently he began punishing this "enemy," eating less and less and refusing other youthful activities that would have developed his body. He began practicing breath control and repeating sacred syllables at home and at the cremation ground "by day and by night." Those around began to pity and scorn this youth who had been born so high and had now fallen so low in worldly terms. Kasahinath too became disillusioned about himself.

When Kasahinath was 14 his family decided he should be married. Though he protested that he could not support himself, and certainly not a wife, his parents perhaps thought that responsibility would help him mend his ways. They married him to a girl of eight, but married life only worsened his despondency. A few months later he ran away from home and found shelter with friends of the family. Only when a letter arrived, explaining that his mother was seriously ill, did he return home. It was shortly after this that his first child-wife died, and within a few weeks his family saw him married again, this time to a girl aged nine. He managed another year with his family, but after this felt compelled to depart, leaving his wife with his relatives. Living with hungry beggars and other outcasts in a temple on the outskirts of Poona he shared with his fellow beggars food that he begged from house to house. He journeyed to another community, and then at age 19, four years following his second marriage, he decided to return home.

Kasahinath's homeward journey took him past a cliff, and as he looked up its side he espied a small cave. He reflected that up there would be an ideal place for him to fast until he died. Up there alone he could wait without food or drink for death to come and bring an end to his misery. He spent two days in the cave without drink, food, or sleep, and then the thought occurred that while waiting to die he should think of God. He began silently to repeat sacred syllables and while doing so became unconscious. When he regained consciousness he saw the figure of someone standing by his side pulling away skin from his physical body. With the shock of this realization he became conscious of an intense thirst. He was so stiff he could make no movement except with his right forearm. Pain was intense and he slipped again into unconsciousness. Eventually he fought his way back to consciousness and found this time that a thunderstorm outside the cave was sending in a stream of water. With his left hand he scooped up water, quenched his thirst, and then began to massage his body to restore feeling.

After three days he saw a Hindu and a Muslim by his side pulling off his entire skin, thus fully revealing his divinely glowing body within. Pointing to that body they declared that they would not let him die. Convinced now that he had a divine mission in life yet to fulfill, he decided to leave the cave. With great difficulty because of his weakness he slid down to the base of the cliff and half crawled to the village of a nearby aboriginal tribe which gave him food. By now he had been gone from home a long time because of his many months in the cave in deep unconsciousness.

On this occasion when he returned home he was received

as an individual who had attained great power through spiritual discipline. His grandfather became ill, and after preparing medicine for him and nursing him Kasahinath decided to take up medicine as a profession. Meanwhile his second wife died, and so he married a third, whom he took with him in departure from their home for his study of medicine.

During the next ten years he earned great wealth from the practice of medicine and buying of real estate, but because of government taxes and lack of business acumen he lost all this. He and his wife set out on a pilgrimage, visiting holy shrines, and at one of these Kasahinath decided to revive his old practice of breath control. His wife noticed him lying unconscious, evidently not even breathing. Though she threw water on his face and restored him to consciousness, his normal breathing did not return, and with great difficulty she managed to get him back home. Concluding that her husband's illness might be because of her evil karma created in a previous existence, she walked around a sacred fig tree 125,000 times. When even this did not seem to help she decided to seek out a yogi who could cure him.

The first yogi that they approached suggested that Kasahinath go to the Spiritual Master named Sai Baba at Shirdi, for further learning in his religious life. But Kasahinath, as a Brahmin, refused such advice to go to Sai Baba, whom he assumed to be a Muslim. Soon after this he met an old man who advised him, instead of drinking cold water, to drink only water that was as hot as his tongue could stand. After Kasahinath refused this advice, he entered into a trance. On the eighth day he saw a stream and knelt to drink. Suddenly he saw this same old man, who this time angrily reminded him of the earlier advice to drink only hot water. The old man disappeared as Kasahinath followed the advice this time. Finding this practice salutary, he followed it throughout the rest of his life.

Advised again by a yogi to visit Sai Baba, at last Kasahinath complied, arriving in Shirdi in 1911. The events that followed bore out the widespread Hindu axiom that a disciple does not select his guru, but that a guru selects his disciple. This applied now as Sai Baba told Kasahinath that it was Sai Baba himself who had been the old man and that in fact Sai Baba for a long time had been responsible for Kasahinath's actions. For

India has been called a structure of diversity cemented by religion. The same nation that boasts this elaborate Hindu art, the bronze statue of the Shiva God of Dance above and the temple carvings below, also found room for a Baba Maharaj who for three years imprisoned himself in a bamboo cage.

one period under the guidance of Sai Baba at Shirdi, a full year, Kasahinath ate no food at all, again showing his contempt for the body that housed his real self. As a result, he passed through stages resembling insanity during which he saw visions and physical objects around him assume myriads of fantastic shapes.

After four years Sai Baba instructed that Kasahinath be religiously worshipped with the same fervor that he himself was worshipped. Henceforth Kasahinath became known as Upasani Baba or Upasani Maharaj. But Upasani Baba had not yet reached full spiritual advancement. He must fully overcome the three basic urges: egotism, love of possessions, and the sex urge. Sai Baba helped him overcome these urges by making various tempting visions appear in front of Upasani Baba and by making him endure a number of difficult tests. Finally Sai Baba was able to tell Upasani that there was no difference between the two of them. After he had conquered, assisted by Sai Baba, the three urges, the fame of Upasani Baba spread as did the reported number of his miracles. He became known for healing physical afflictions, casting out evil spirits, and solving financial problems. But perhaps his best known miracle involved invisibility.

A hostile group of Brahmins arrived to do him harm, and upon their approach Upasani made himself and those around him invisible. The Brahmins were informed that because they were unpure they could not see Upasani Baba. On another occasion he fed thirty devotees orange slices from a single orange.

Upasani described himself as the ancient one, divinely eternal, who is everything. In this modern incarnation he became best known for his long years of self-inflicted suffering, including a three-year period in his later life when he imprisoned himself in a small cage of bamboo canes, a self-made prison he never left even momentarily. Though at last he left his physical body on December 24, 1941, his numerous devotees consider his real self closer to them now than ever before.

A Nightly View Of Cosmic Suffering

**ORAL ROBERTS (A.D. January 24, 1918-   ).
U.S.A. Oklahoma. A farm near Ada.**

Before his birth Oral's mother asked God to give her a son who would become a minister. In addition she made a vow to give her unborn son to God in exchange for the healing of a neighbor's child dying of pneumonia. Oral was the youngest of five children born to Ellis and Claudius Roberts, devout members of the Pentecostal Holiness Church. Ellis Roberts was a part-Indian farmer who took up preaching shortly before Oral's birth, and Oral's mother also was part Indian. They named the future famed healer and educator Granville Oral Roberts but called him Oral. As Oral himself later explained, he stammered and stuttered so much as a child it was ironic that he be called Oral. While a baby he also had the problem of walking only on the sides of his little feet until his mother took the problem to God. Other problems continued with Oral throughout his youth, however, one of these being his awkwardness and shyness. Schoolmates teased him because of his inability to speak properly, and on one occasion laughter at his affliction became so excruciatingly embarrassing that he hid under his house until the guests left.

At age 16 Oral decided to move out from under parental discipline and a religious regimen never really accepted by him and went to the nearby town of Atoka. There he found work as a handyman and lodging in the home of a judge. Though he delivered papers and worked in a grocery store on Saturdays, he maintained a high grade average in school. But despite the good turn of events, the 16-year-old youth collapsed on a gymnasium floor in the final minutes of a basketball game. Unconscious, with blood hemorrhaging from his mouth, he was rushed back to the relative security of his parents' home. Doctors diagnosed advanced tuberculosis in both lungs and advised that he enter a sanitarium at once. While waiting for an available hospital bed for the youth, relatives and other friends prayed for his salvation and healing. Eventually Oral decided that the devil had afflicted his body, and he himself prayed long prayers that he would be saved, finally promising, "Lord, I will preach the Gospel." Shortly after this he felt "the presence of Jesus Christ enter my feet and my entire body began to quiver." But though he had reached a spiritual plateau, his physical body still remained in the depths of serious illness.

Not long after Oral's body began to quiver because of the presence of Jesus, his older brother Elmer hurried to his room and told of a tent revivalist in Ada who was healing the sick in a miraculous way. Assisted by his parents Elmer carried his younger brother to a borrowed car and headed out over the country roads to the revival tent. On the way, as Oral testified later, God's voice spoke clearly to him, saying, "Son, I am going to heal you and you are to take the message of my healing power to your generation."

At the revival tent, supported by pillows in a rocking chair, when it was Oral's time they took him up front to the evangelist. The evangelist said a short prayer, "Thou foul disease. I command you in the name of Jesus Christ to come out of this boy's lungs. Loose him and let him go." What happened next began a series of events in Oral's life that the evangelist describes as continually unfolding. "A blinding flash engulfed me and that light was all I could see for several moments. Like the night I was converted, I felt light as a feather, only this time it was in my body that I felt the sudden impact of divine power." The next thing the youth knew he was racing back and forth on the platform shouting at the top of his voice, "I am healed! I am healed!" In addition to the instantaneous healing of his tuberculosis, he found that his stuttering also was instantly cured.

A few weeks after his recovery Oral was ordained in the Pentecostal Holiness Church. With another young preacher he

63

began conducting a summer revival, and then at the end of the summer Oral joined his father to form an active father-son evangelistic team. Though the father and son combination was successful, when his father accepted the pastorate of a church in Westville, Oklahoma, his son continued on in the evangelistic field by himself. Then in 1936, young, tall, and handsome, Oral met a beautiful, religious girl, Evelyn Lutman, who was playing a guitar at a camp meeting in Sulphur, Oklahoma, and on Christmas Day 1938 Oral's father married the two in his church in Westville.

For a decade after their marriage the couple traveled from one revival or small pastorate to another. Oral considers this his decade of intense and often painful preparation. At the end of the decade, in 1946, while pastoring at a small church in Toccoa, Georgia, he had an experience that convinced him his "hour" was near. A deacon in Oral's church dropped a heavy motor, almost severing a foot. Oral and another deacon rushed to the garage where the victim was in such pain he was thrashing about on the floor. Roberts said later that the deacon "could only point at his foot in an unspoken plea for me to pray." Oral touched the end of the victim's toe with his right hand and cried, "Jesus, heal!" The man stopped rolling in agony on the floor and asked, "Oral, what did you do to me?" His pastor answered, "Nothing, Clyde, except pray." But the nothing resulted in a cry from the floor. "I'm healed." Proving it the fallen man took off his shoe, stood up, stamped his foot on the floor, with no swelling or pain left. His foot had been instantly restored. The noninjured deacon who had accompanied Oral to the scene of the accident regained his composure enough to exclaim to his pastor, "If you could have God's power to pray like that all the time, you could be used of God to bring a revival to the world."

That miracle in Taccoa, accompanied by the deacon's prophecy about the worldwide ministry, reminded Oral of the fact that at his birth his mother had given him to God. Yet though it all seemed part of a pattern that he saw developing "according to the divine plan," he felt that he had not quite reached enough victory—that in fact "God had reserved some important lessons for me to learn." He returned to Oklahoma where, despite two children now also to feed, early in 1947 in

Enid, Oklahoma, he found himself not only pastoring the Pentecostal Holiness Church but at the same time attending school at Phillips University there. He studied and prayed. Then he decided to fast and in doing so lost a great deal of weight. God kept telling him inside, "Don't be like others, be like Jesus." Leaving the house early one morning, in haste to get to a college class, he realized he had forgotten his daily morning reading of a passage of scripture and a prayer to God for the day. He returned to his house, opened the Bible at random, and began to read where his glance fell. The passage he saw was in the third epistle of John, verse 2, from the New Testament of the Bible, "Beloved, I wish above all things that thou mayest prosper and be in health, even as thy soul prospereth." He read the passage over and over, sensing for the first time the full concept of abundant life on earth, in conjunction with enriching of the soul, a theme that would become a central message in his forthcoming worldwide evangelism.

Despite the impact of reading III John that morning, and similar passages on other occasions, in his search for special power from God he realized that he still had farther to go. God yet had things to show him before he suffered through to his ultimate achievement. One night his wife discovered Oral in the corner of a room, on his knees, sobbing and praying. When she asked him about his strange actions he said that he had been experiencing the same distressing dream, night after night. "I dream that God shows me mankind as he sees them and hears them. What I see and hear takes my breath away. Evelyn, I did not know this before this dream, but most of the people in this world are sick or afraid in some way." He added that, "These people are lost and helpless. They must have healing from God." Roberts explained later that the dream always was the same: "millions of people crying out for healing and help...the whole human race crying out to God for healing." Later he explained, "After 25 years of being in the arena with suffering people, I know that what I experienced in 1947 was more than a dream."

Yet despite the vividness of what he had seen in early 1947, Oral felt that now at age 29 and a half years, clearly approaching a spiritual breakthrough, he yet must have one thing more. "I must have God's annointing to pray for the sick." He

*This 500-acre campus of Oral Roberts University in Tulsa, Okla-
homa, represents an investment of more than $150 million. Its
campus Prayer Tower operates 24 hours a day and handles more
than a half million calls for prayer each year.*

had to make direct contact with the Lord, "to hear His voice
again and receive my instructions." He went to his church,
locked himself in his study, and proceeded to address the Lord:
"Today is the end of my searching. I am going to find You. I
will lie down on this floor before You and start praying. I will
never rise until you speak to me . . . . Suddenly, God spoke to
me in an audible voice . . . . 'From this hour you will heal the
sick and cast out devils by My power.'"

From that day of his annointing from God the Oral Roberts worldwide evangelism has become probably the best known
living legend in the so-called modern faith healing movement. A
pioneer in using both worldwide radio and television effectively,

Oral Roberts, shown here, is the author of more than 50 books, has the largest United States television viewing audience of any syndicated Sunday religious program, is the founder and president of Oral Roberts University, has been named "Oklahoman of the Year," and is a member of the Oklahoma Hall Of Fame.

as early as 1956 he already was conducting services over 300 radio and 115 television stations. He discovered a warmth—a feeling of God's presence—in his right hand, and very little or none in the left. Therefore his right hand has been termed his point of contact in healing. He has asked millions of radio listeners to touch their radio as he tells them "Something good is going to happen to you today." He asks television viewers to reach toward his hands on the screen and explains that "God heals!" He personally has laid hands on hundreds of thousands of afflicted, from top movie stars in Hollywood, U.S.A., to darkest Africa's deplorable lepers that he had to force himself to touch.

It is said that strangeness breeds fear and, as with all things unordinary, Roberts has been severely criticized, great criticism matching his increasing sphere of influence. The articulate worldwide evangelist has collected millions of dollars and in many ways has lived in the traditional style of millionaires, a long way from the sickly, stuttering child on an Oklahoma farm. When he left the Pentecostal Holiness Church and joined the Methodist Church, because he felt led to, he was accused of forsaking fundamental Christianity and going religiously modern. When he forsook his evangelistic healing campaigns and concentrated upon the large and now thriving Oral Roberts University in Tulsa, Oklahoma, he was accused similarly. When he began an almost unbelievable mammoth campaign to establish at his campus in Tulsa one of the world's greatest hospitals, a skeptic asked on nationwide television why Oral Roberts needed a hospital anyway if his hands still had their healing power.

Yet, as throughout his adult life, he meets such criticism either with silence or with only mild rejoinder. Instead, his point of contact has remained, as it was when he addressed the United States Democratic National Convention in 1972, to call upon God "to heal." That is why he is considered, perhaps more than any other, to have accomplished most toward making miracle healing respectable in modern times. (Many publications about the life of Oral Roberts including autobiographies have been published in Tulsa, Oklahoma. Probably best known and most comprehensive is *My Story*, Oral Roberts, Tulsa, 1961. An Oral Roberts autobiography published elsewhere is *The Call,* Doubleday & Company, New York, 1972. For an interesting account of Oral Roberts compared with eight other ministers read *The Preachers*, James Morris, St. Martins Press, New York, 1973.)

Overpowering Millions Of Afflictions In Spite Of Oneself

KATHRYN KUHLMAN (A.D. May 9, 1907-February 20, 1976). U.S.A. Missouri. Five miles south of Concordia.

Born into a prosperous farming and merchandising family of German extraction, she was the youngest among two daughters and a son. Red-headed young Kathryn found herself the daughter of a nonreligious father, whom she adored, and a less-adorable church-going Baptist mother. Though her father became mayor of Concordia and widely respected, he announced often that he despised preachers, saying they were all "in it for the money." Out of this environment in 1913 Kathryn's older sister married a traveling young evangelist, her older brother earned a teen-age reputation for wildness that included widely rumored thievery, and in 1921 at age 14 Kathryn faced a decision between the two disparate life styles. The attractive but fiery young redhead had a reputation that her mother described as "flirty" and otherwise suggested that her choice of the alternatives would be the nonreligious.

Kathryn's many mischievous pranks, for which her strict mother would soundly spank her, included, for example, at age nine plugging and thereby ruining more than a hundred melons in her grandfather's melon patch. And that same year she went from house to house in Concordia and, unknown to her fastidious mother, invited 30 of the town's most prominent women to each bring a cake and surprise her disheveled mother on wash-day Monday, her mother's birthday. Each crime was successful and each subsequent spanking by her mother was successfully

69

severe. But when a visiting Baptist evangelist held a protracted revival meeting at the local Methodist church Kathryn attended all one week. Then Sunday morning she answered the minister's altar call to come forward and be "born again." After this she had the experience of floating rather than walking home with her mother from the service. When she arrived home she told her father, "Papa, something's happened to me. Jesus has come into my heart," but he merely stared, then replied without emotion, "I'm glad," and walked away. Throughout her life she was never sure if he understood her, and a continuing sorrow was that to her knowledge her father never in his lifetime accepted Christ.

At 16 Kathryn had all the public education available in Concordia, and she left town to join the tent-and-sawdust travel circuit of her sister and evangelist brother-in-law. She stayed with them a half-dozen years, whistle-stopping and primarily tent-appearing in one community after another in the western and far-western United States. Then she decided to strike out on her own and preached her first sermon in Boise, Idaho, in a small run-down mission in a poor section of the city. In parting, Kathryn asked her sister for a loan of $10 to buy a new yellow dress in which to preach her first sermon. Kathryn's sister and evangelist husband had less than $10 in their bank account, and though Kathryn accepted the check she agreed to hold it until at some future date they could cover it and make it good. Meanwhile she cajoled a local merchant into letting her have a yellow dress on credit, a debt subsequently repaid in full. She had a piano wheeled in from the bar next door and rickety chairs brought in along with a makeshift pulpit. But despite the yellow dress and the success of having preached her first sermon, finances for a long time proved a problem for Kathryn as well as her sister and brother-in-law. In one western town she slept for three nights in a swept-out turkey house.

Yet because of the energy and persistence of the attractive young evangelist, plus business acumen learned from her father abetted by plentiful use of advertising that included posters and handbills, gradually results appeared. Into the late hours of the night, after the end of the formal service, she would counsel all those seeking more religious instruction. In Joliet, Illinois, during one of these late sessions she had her first experience with

These two photographs show Kathryn Kuhlman during the early years of her ministry.

the phenomenon known as "speaking in tongues." Among the few who lingered from the departing crowd of several hundred was a young woman school teacher from Chicago attending with her mother. The teacher suddenly knelt, lifted her face toward the ceiling, and in the most beautiful voice Kathryn had ever heard began singing in a strange language. The young teacher's mother gasped that the singer could not be her daughter because, "Isabel can't even carry a tune. My daughter can't sing a note." But the young teacher, who had never heard of the "gift of tongues," actually had been singing in the unknown tongue, even though afterwards she was as amazed at what had happened as were her mother and Kathryn.

After spending six months preaching in an old Montgomery Ward building in Pueblo, Colorado, Kathryn moved in 1933 to an old Montgomery Ward building in Denver, Colorado. Only 125 attended the first night of the campaign, but 400 came the following night, and from then on the old warehouse could not hold the crowds. She began inviting visiting evangelists, some of whom practiced "divine healing," exposing Kathryn fully at last to this phenomenon. Though she seldom prayed for the sick, she was gratified as well as amazed to see others healed. She spent a spectacular five years in Denver, during which she moved to larger headquarters and nightly began preaching to an overflow crowd which walked in under a huge sign that read "Denver Revival Tabernacle" and smaller signs that read "Evangelist Kathryn Kuhlman" and "Prayer Changes Things." At the close of each service to these crowds of several thousand she went on the radio, live, for a program entitled "Smiling Through."

It was at the end of five years in Denver that Kathryn Kuhlman made the error of falling in love with a handsome but married visiting young evangelist, who divorced his wife and left her and his two sons to marry evangelist Kathryn Kuhlman. The resultant notoriety forced them both from Denver and effectively ended their ministry for the six years they lived together. Though they were deeply in love with each other it was at the expense of their spiritual and economic life. As they prayed for forgiveness and at the same time tried to rationalize their guilt they had to try and seek out small towns for evangelism where they were not known. After they separated Kathryn said tearfully, "No one will ever know what this ministry has cost me. Only Jesus . . . I had to make a choice. Would I serve the man I loved or the God I loved?"

But on this crucible of human despair Kathryn established a startling new ministry built on prayer, reading of the Bible, and "power of the Holy Spirit" and "the saving Grace of Christ crucified." Though she never considered herself a healer and instead preached only "the power of the Holy Spirit" rather than "preached healing," almost from the first, after her six years of spiritual exile, miraculous healings at her services became commonplace and her fame worldwide. Her ministry, headquartered in Pittsburgh, Pennsylvania, lasted from 1950 until her death from heart failure in 1976 at age 68. Between her radio and personal ministry emanating from her headquarters in Carnegie Hall in Pittsburgh and her long-lasting CBS television and personal ministry to hundreds of thousands in California, an estimated three million people were cured of some affliction because of her ministry.

Though thousands reported cures through her radio and television messages, something about her personal presence, "the personal power of the Holy Spirit," always seemed most effective. On numerous occasions she would simply look toward one or more people, some in groups of several hundred, and the knees of one and all would buckle and their owners slump to the floor. U. S. General of the Army Omar Bradley came to her service, and when she faced him he was thus "slain by the Spirit" once and as soon as he was helped to his feet he was at once "slain by the Spirit" again. Those healed ranged from the unknown to the known, including actor Robert Young of the "Marcus Welby, M.D" television series. Famed faith-healer and educator Oral Roberts visited one of her services and afterwards told her that "You have something I don't have, and I've never had." He explained later that he had always found it advisable to use both his voice and physical touch in healing, whereas all that Kathryn Kuhlman needed was to be in the presence of someone in order to be effective. The first honorary doctorate awarded by Oral Roberts University in Tulsa, Oklahoma, was in 1973 to Kathryn Kuhlman.

Certainly evangelist Kathryn Kuhlman had many critics as well as followers. Her enterprise definitely was big business. In

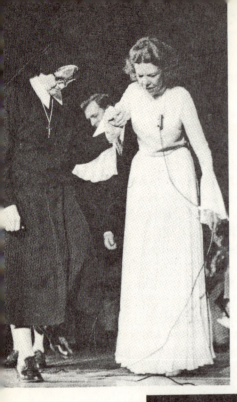

*Kathryn Kuhlman in a "miracle service"
in St. Louis, Missouri, in 1975.*

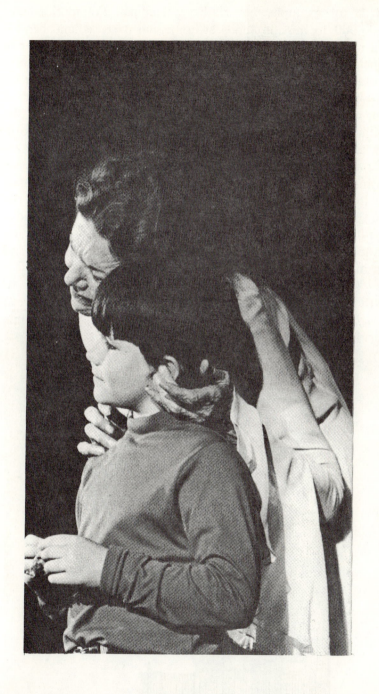

1972, for example, her Kathryn Kuhlman Foundation gave $500,000 to mission funds at home and overseas, and her TV and radio ministry already was exceeding $1,500,000. In her financially successful years she had a life style of Cadillacs, Continentals, and Lear jets plus many expensive gifts given her by fans and a personal wardrobe that cost thousands of dollars—a long way from a farm six miles outside Concordia, Missouri. She had a manner of speaking that seemed overly dramatic and otherwise affected, she ran her organization in a single-handed autocratic way, involved herself in several legal controversies with business associates, and she always seemed much too impressed by famous personalities. But not since the time of John the Baptist who preceded Christ has there been such miraculous manifestation of the Power of the Holy Spirit from such an unorthodox human mechanism—it is said by her biographers and her millions of followers to this day.

(For a fascinating and highly informative biography of Kathryn Kuhlman written by an associate and friend read *Daughter of Destiny: Kathryn Kuhlman...Her Story*, Jamie Buckingham, Logos International, 1976.)

Past Foreign Physicians Practice Future Medicine In Brazil

ARIGO (A.D. October 18, 1918-January 11, 1971). Brazil. Farm near the village of Congonhas do Campo.

Antonio de Freitas Sobrinho, father of Arigo, was a hard-working Brazilian farmer. As one of the town fathers of Congonhas do Campo, he was a community leader who served on the board of the town council, sometimes as its chairman. He fathered eight sons, one of whom he named Jose Pedro de Freitas. Jose Pedro de Freitas soon earned the good-natured name of Arigo, a Brazilian word that translates as jovial country hick. Though Arigo was quite popular, family members seemed to be succeeding in life while he was not. As his brothers in school enhanced the family's reputation, one eventually becoming an attorney and another a priest, and as other relatives gained wealth, Arigo labored three years at school and then dropped out. A powerful youth he worked full time on his father's farm except when fraternizing with his increasing circle of friends. But all this did not preclude a spiritual life as he worshipped devoutly with family members at the Catholic Church of Bom Jesus do Matosinho, high on a steep hill overlooking the town.

The crude country youth found his religious life enlivened with a series of supernatural experiences. During three years in school and later on he became bothered at times by a round, bright light, "so brilliant that it nearly blinded me." On occasion also he heard a voice speaking to him in a strange guttural language. But both kinds of experiences were infrequent, and he learned to accept them without belaboring the fact to others.

Anyway, the supernatural is more widely accepted in Brazil than in many countries of the world. A large country ranging from Amazon jungles to large cities such as Sao Paulo, with a population near eight million, the nation seems spiritually glued. About 90 percent of the Brazilians claim allegiance to the Catholic church. In addition, all major economic and social strata throughout the country have hundreds of thousands of believers in spiritualism or spiritism, "the belief that the dead survive as spirits which can communicate with the living, especially with the help of a medium."

In an environment of strict Catholicism on one hand and spiritualism on the other, Arigo's infrequent experiences with strange lights and words were acceptable. In this spiritual garden of flowers Arigo continued to mature as a rough brier. He became known for his strength and his coarseness, his "four-letter" words at times considered coarse even for the countryside's vernacular. The powerful youth emerged from his father's farm to begin working in a neighborhood iron mine and in 1943 married his fourth cousin Arlete Andre. She also was Catholic, and as far as is known did not practice spiritualism, a belief frowned upon by the church.

Work at the mine was anything but pleasure. Arigo and most of his fellow miners would rise about three in the morning, walk almost seven and a half miles, and work brutally all day for a pittance. The situation led to the miners' resentment. Because of his popularity, resulting from his jovial good nature and reputation for generosity to his friends and other neighbors, Arigo was elected the union's president and led the union in a strike. As a result of the unsuccessful strike Arigo was fired, but continued trying to help his fellow miners as a nonemployee. His wife stood devotedly by him, helping support the growing family as a seamstress, and then his father helped establish him in a combined tavern-restaurant business known as the Bar do Arigo. Though his popularity brought good trade to the business, his generous habit of giving food to strangers as well as friends, and extending credit or money to both, assured continued financial problems for the rapidly growing family.

Increasing with his problems as a family provider came another increasing problem for Arigo as persistent dreams began plaguing him. In them reoccurred that same guttural speech that sounded like German, which he could not understand. At times accompanying his dreams came stultifying headaches which he experienced physically upon awakening. The terrible experiences became so persistent he found himself dreading nighttime. He tried not to disturb his wife, instead dressing and slipping out to walk the streets of the town as he wore down the pain. At other times she would awaken to find him in the bed beside her sobbing in agony. One night the dream clarified, showing a group of doctors and nurses in surgical gowns; a somewhat stout, bald man was directing the operation of a patient on a table, and this head doctor was speaking in the same tone and guttural accent that had plagued Arigo so long. Night after night the experience reoccurred until Arigo no longer could separate it from actuality. Only in the daytime did he seem to shake off its effects, by wholeheartedly branching into fairly successful businesses such as real estate and used car selling, and by ascending to the Church of Bom Jesus to pray.

Then one night the stout, bald-headed doctor identified himself as Dr. Adolpho Fritz who had died during World War I before his mission in life was completed. After studying Arigo's generosity and love for mankind, Dr. Fritz had selected him to continue the doctor's work on this earth, assisted by others who had been doctors before they died. Dr. Fritz added that to obtain peace Arigo was to begin helping afflicted who needed his help, the procedure being for him to hold a crucifix that he had found earlier on his father's farm. It all was so real, Arigo leaped from his bed with a scream and went racing through the town's streets naked. A crowd gathered, including his wife, and they managed to placate the sobbing, incoherent man enough to lead him home. The family doctor was summoned to the home and, finding nothing physically wrong, suggested prompt psychiatric treatment, a diagnosis to which Arigo agreed with readiness. What followed, as Arigo continued refusing the advice of the German Dr. Fritz, was a series of visits to physicians and psychiatrists and even an official attempt by the Catholic church to exorcise whatever evil spirits might be possessing him. Yet Arigo's nightmarish nights and now days continued.

Then one day a crippled friend met Arigo, and almost before he realized it Arigo heard himself give the brusque advice, "It's time you got rid of those crutches." With impatience he

79

grabbed the man's crutches from him and told him to walk, whereupon the man obeyed and continued to walk unassisted. After this Arigo was successful in commanding other friends to be well, and his own headaches and nightmares ceased during this era. However, resulting criticism from the church and other skeptics brought him deep distress. Arigo's parish priest came to him promptly and reminded him with sharpness that spiritism was in direct conflict with the church. Confronted by all his criticism, Arigo confessed to his error in bowing to Dr. Fritz's wishes and agreed to stop. On his door he even erected a prominent sign with the words:

IN THIS HOUSE WE ARE ALL CATHOLICS
SPIRITISM IS A THING OF THE DEVIL.

The only thing was, as Arigo gave in to his criticism his headaches returned with a vengeance and included prolonged daytime blackouts. More trips to physicians and psychiatrists were merely followed by greater insistance from Dr. Fritz.

But in 1950, at the age of 32, Arigo's life took an irrevocable step forward in the direction of supernatural healing. A senator was running for reelection, and though his doctor warned him that he was critically ill with lung cancer and should hurry to the United States for an operation, the politically eager senator determined to wait until after the election instead. In lieu of surgery he waged a campaign with all the vigor he could, including a campaign swing to the rather isolated area of Brazil where Arigo lived. One night the senator lay tossing on his hotel bed and was on the verge of dropping off to sleep when Arigo entered his room holding a razor in his hand. Though Arigo's eyes were glazed with a vacant faraway look, the amazed speechless senator surprisingly felt no fear. The senator heard Arigo's voice in a thick German accent declaring that because of the emergency there would have to be an operation, and then the senator blacked out. Though Arigo himself never remembered the event, the senator of course remembered him well, especially after awakening to find blood on his slashed pajama top as well as blood already clotted over a professional looking incision along his rib cage. The apprehensive and distraught senator hurried to the next plane to Rio to see his doctor. The doctor thoroughly examined the successful operation with x-rays and surmised, until enlightened by the senator, that his patient had just returned after unexpectedly taking his advice to hurry to the United States for the hoped-for life-saving surgery.

The popular senator saw to it that Arigo's name became a household word in much of Brazil almost overnight. Arigo's next supernatural surgery occurred soon and in some ways was even more spectacular. A friend of the family was in bed with neighbors gathered around awaiting her death at any minute from cancer of the uterus. The priest had already arrived in the candle-lit room, administered the last rites of the church, and left. But when Arigo and his wife Arlete called to pay their last respects to the dying woman, Arigo with his head bowed in silent prayer began to experience a feeling that was becoming familiar to him. A tingling that began in his head and eased down through his legs was accompanied by a trembling of his body and his eyes clouding. Without warning he rushed into the kitchen and rushed back bringing a large kitchen knife. With a commanding voice he ordered the group, already riveted with terror, to keep back, and then pulled aside the sheets and plunged the knife into the woman's vagina and began probing. Though one woman relative ran screaming from the room the other visitors remained in place, and the dying woman herself remained restful in apparent calm as Arigo continued to jab the blade. Then he removed the blade, shoved in his hand, and pulled out a huge uterine tumor about a half-foot in diameter. With this he strode into the kitchen, dropped the bloody knife and bloodier mass of flesh into the sink, and sat down on a chair and began sobbing.

When that surgery also proved successful, the woman recovering as completely as the senator a brief time earlier, Arigo with initial bewilderment that seemed a long time dissipating began healing the patients who now lined up by the hundreds outside his door. During the ensuing days of long incessant work Arigo remembered little; either of writing complicated prescriptions in technical pharmacy language or of simply giving verbal advice that proved curative with amazing accuracy; or of the numerous operations he performed with a kitchen knife, pocket knife, or household scissors. He could stop the flow of blood with a verbal request to Jesus and could accurately diagnose disease or read blood pressures by merely glancing at a patient.

As might be expected, home life as such in the house disintegrated. Arigo refused to charge or even accept any gifts whatsoever, explaining that "Jesus never charged for what he did." But even when he had to leave the house to work at one of his jobs to keep the family from bankruptcy, the crowds came and waited. It became advisable to shift the clinic to an abandoned church across the street from Arigo's house. The church again became a center for religious power. Arigo credited Jesus as enabling him to use the skilled experience of Dr. Fritz and the other long-dead physicians. One of several crude signs on Arigo's clinic walls read:

DON'T LEAN AGAINST THE WALL
THINK OF JESUS
WAIT IN AN ORDERLY WAY

In all of Brazil the healer became one of about a half dozen best known personalities. His healings, including his surgery, were the subject of detailed photography preserved in color motion pictures as well as black-and-white photography. A locally, respected spiritist group claimed independently that through a medium Dr. Fritz had revealed that he, indeed, and other deceased physicians had chosen Arigo as their present-day vehicle, and that Dr. Fritz had spent 16 years preparing Arigo to carry on the healing work. Not only the meek but the mighty came to Arigo, including the daughter of Brazil's president as well as other well knowns from outside and inside Brazil. Yet the very fame that came to Arigo forced reaction from the Catholic church as well as legal and medical authorities in Brazil. Spiritism was a heresy, and practicing medicine without a license was illegal and of course contrary to the best interests of the Brazilian medical association. Incredibly, despite fame and acclaim now worldwide, Arigo on more than one occasion suffered lengthy trials in Brazilian courts, each time resulting in jail sentences of at least several months. Despite the fact that a number of leading clergymen and jurists, even including the judge who tried him and the prison officials who imprisoned him, were sympathetic, the church and legal strictures were too unyielding

Arigo.

to be circumvented in Arigo's case.

Even though Arigo at last put all his legal problems behind him and resumed his healing mission full force, the sustained aggressiveness that cost him many months in jail also cost his life in middle age. Despite his own publicly voiced predictions of his impending death, coupled with his long-held knowledge that he took continual chances with aggressive driving on Brazil's mountain highways, he drove too rapidly on a curving rain-slicked mountain road not far from his home. As a result Arigo in the second week of January 1971 was one among several who died in a crash with an oncoming car. Someone cried out in despair that Arigo's home town had been orphaned. The same could be said for the thousands of afflicted who had been hoping for a visit to Brazil's most famous healer in world history, documented in detail including still and movie photography. (For a fascinating well-documented and well-indexed work about the intriguing life of Arigo read: *ARIGO: Surgeon of the Rusty Knife*, John G. Fuller, Thomas Y. Crowell Company, 1974.)

Present-Tense Conversations With Past History-Makers

SRI RAMAKRISHNA (A.D. February 18, 1836-August 16, 1886). Bengal. Kamarpukur.

Born into a devout Brahmin family the child received the name Gadadhar Chattopadhyaya. At age seven Gadadhar had the first of a lifetime of remarkable experiences. While outside one day he saw some snow-white cranes pass in front of a dark thundercloud. The majesty of the contrast overcame him and, falling immediately into an unconscious state, he dropped to the ground. A passing neighbor carried the unconscious youth home. The villagers predicted a religious career for him, and the youth never went to school, remaining illiterate to the end of his life. Instead of school it was life in his brother's footsteps, the life of a priest. When he was 23 his relatives arranged his marriage to a five-year-old child bride. As happened often in India with the marriages of spiritual leaders, even when his child bride became old enough, their marriage throughout life was never consummated physically.

In the temple Gadadhar developed an overriding devotion to the image of Lord Krishna, an incarnation of the Hindu god Vishnu. He began to believe that the image of Lord Krishna was in reality Lord Krishna himself, a physical manifestation to be put to bed and awakened and bathed and fed and clothed. He also paid unusual devotion to another Hindu god, Rama. A monkey had been an important animal in the god Rama's past, and so Gadadhar began to walk like a monkey, so much so that the lower end of his spine lengthened an inch. He wore only a loincloth and moved about in jumps. He preferred to eat fruits and nuts and did not like the fruits to be peeled.

People combined the names of Gadadhar's two objects of worship, the god Rama and Lord Krishna, and thus Gadadhar became known as Ramakrishna. He began to believe that all religions lead their devotees to the same one God, no matter what the path, as in another culture all roads were said to lead to Rome. Ramakrishna also decided to test his belief by experimenting in other religions. He dressed as a Muslim, repeated the name of Allah, and after three days saw the radiant figure of Muhammad appear in front of his eyes. The figure approached Ramakrishna and talked with him and lost himself in Ramakrishna himself. Eight years later Ramakrishna approached Christianity with the same fervor as he had the Islamic religion, listening to readings from the Bible, finding himself engrossed with Jesus' life and teachings. One day a picture of the Madonna and Child came to life in his presence, and three days later as he walked in a garden a man with beautiful large eyes, serene countenance, and fair skin approached him and talked with him. He recognized the other as Jesus, and Jesus too became one with Ramakrishna. Ramakrishna concluded, as do the many thousands of his followers today, that all religions lead to the same God, Ramakrishna Himself.

On August 16, 1886, Ramakrishna smiled at those about him and then went into that unconscious state in which God on earth leaves the physical body, never to return. The following Christmas Eve after Ramakrishna's death his disciples founded the Ramakrishna Order, their mission to become Christs themselves, to aid in the redemption of the world.

This is one of a series of 22 elaborate shrines built about A.D. 1000 in the same India in which Sri Ramakrishna because of his faith would live like a monkey and leader Sathya Sai Baba would produce gold coins from his mouth for the same reason.

Producing Gold Coins From One's Mouth

SATHYA SAI BABA (A.D. November 23, 1926-   ).
India. Puttaparthi.

His parents practiced Hinduism devoutly in a small village. At birth named Sathyanarayana Raju, various miraculous events were associated with this nativity. An ensemble of musical instruments played by unseen hands sounded in the house, announcing his birth. Under the bed of this newborn child a mysterious cobra appeared. At an early age the child showed greatly advanced knowledge and began giving advanced instructions to his own teachers. Also, early on he began gaining a reputation for miraculous powers. For example, by simply reaching into empty school bags he could bring forth pencils and candy or cookies for the delight of his classmates.

One day his teacher annoyed him, and so Sathyanaray used his miraculous power to keep the teacher pressed into his chair until Sathyanaray released him. He formed a prayer group among his classmates and taught them Hindu scriptures, which he already knew by heart. He wrote religious dramas and had them performed by neighborhood friends. He took sand and formed images of gods and then made them turn into gold at his touch. In early 1940 he entered a trance that lasted for about two months, after which he got up from bed, called together the family members, and from nowhere produced flowers and sweet food which he distributed to them. When the neighbors arrived his miracles continued, as for them he produced rice and milk from the invisible realm. With this he announced that in reality he was Sai Baba of Shirdi reincarnated. Sai Baba had predicted shortly before his death that he would be reincarnated eight years later, a point that many people now remembered. Remembering, people began to flock to Sathyanaray and worship him. He dropped out of school and moved into a nearby temple.

In 1950 on his twenty-fourth birthday his devotees dedicated a spectacular shrine to Sathya Sai Baba, as Sathanaray now was called. From his fourteenth year to the present he has served at this shrine or traveled about India and abroad, serving an increasing number of devotees. His miraculous powers, attested by many devotees, have given him a special worldwide reputation. In addition to healing the physically and mentally afflicted, including the casting out of evil spirits, he converts one type of matter into another, and from a small material object produces large quantities. He vanishes at will, appearing as he wishes anywhere in the world in whatever physical form he desires. He reads minds and motivates minds in the spiritual direction they should take. One of his most widely discussed miracles, witnessed by as many as 50,000 observers each October in India, consists of Sathya Sai Baba drawing from his mouth two gold pieces that he has had formed magically within himself. His devotees consider him the Supreme Power... God on earth in all His manifestations.

Producing Language From Gold

JOSEPH SMITH (A.D. December 23, 1805-June 27, 1844). U.S.A. Vermont. Sharon.

Most of Joseph Smith's forebears were tillers of the soil, except for interruptions from time to time such as soldiering in the colonial and revolutionary wars. In addition to tilling the soil Joseph's grandfather himself was something of a prophet who once made this startling pronouncement: "It has been borne in upon my soul that one of my descendants will promulgate a work to revolutionize the world of religious faith." His grandson Joseph the Prophet was born in Sharon, Vermont, fourth of ten children born to Joseph, Sr., and Lucy Mack Smith. By the time Joseph the Prophet was born in 1805 his father was proving himself such a poor farmer and businessman the family was approaching poverty. By the time Joseph the Prophet was five the family had moved three times in five years in Vermont and New Hampshire, searching in vain for an easier or at least adequate method of making a living at farming. In fact young Joseph the Prophet was born into a lifetime of insecurity that he could not escape during his eventful life of 38 years.

Not only was Joseph the Prophet's life insecure, but he was born into a post-revolutionary war era and area of general insecurity. Stability once associated with England disappeared. Many impoverished New England farmers headed west to seek better times. It was in addition an American era of intense religious excitement in which the Shakers and many other sects

90

featuring religious emotionalism flourished from New England to Kentucky. Though Joseph, Sr., and Lucy both had strong religious leanings, both eventually becoming strong followers of their son Joseph the Prophet, neither had ever been active in any organized religion prior to their son's. Lucy would write in later years that prior to the ascendency of her son, "I spent much of my time in reading the Bible and praying: but, notwithstanding my great anxiety to experience a change of heart, another matter would always interpose in all my meditations—If I remain a member of no church all religious people will say I am of the world; and if I join some one of the different denominations, all the rest will say I am in error." Family inclinations were more toward the Presbyterian and Methodist denominations, young Joseph the Prophet himself favoring the Methodist but questioning all.

The youth of Joseph the Prophet was anything but exemplary and would bring him much criticism throughout the remainder of his life. Though a well-liked youth he earned a reputation for shiftlessness, tall-tales, dabbling in magic arts, and from time to time of looking for buried treasure, a favorite pastime of idlers of that day who were hoping for luck to spare their backs. It was easy for impoverished farm hands to think of buried treasure that would make this furrow the last they ever would plow. Eventually Joseph's first published article about his youth, written for his church newspaper, would be this apology:

At the age of ten my father's family removed to Palmyra, New York, where, and in the vicinity of which, I lived, or, made it my place of residence, until I was twenty-one: the latter part, in the town of Manchester. During this time, as is common to most or all youths, I fell into many vices and follies; but as my accusers are, and have been forward to accuse me of being guilty of gross and outrageous violations of the peace and good order of the community, I take the occasion to remark that, though, as I have said above, "as is common to most, or all youths, I fell into many vices and follies," I have not, neither can it be sustained, in truth, been guilty of wronging or injuring any man or society of men; and those imperfections to which I allude, and for which I have often had occasion to lament, were a light, and too often, vain mind, exhibiting a foolish and trifling conversation.

Regardless of Joseph's apologies his most scholarly critics have agreed that he was likeable and imaginative, and that though uneducated formally, from childhood on he showed remarkable signs of intelligence and leadership. Also, like his mother in particular, he had a strong belief in the power of the supernatural. Once, after digging a well for a neighbor to a distance of 24 feet down, he discovered a type of stone known as a "crystal-gazing" or "seer stone." Afterwards he earned the reputation of being able to look at this stone and define the location of everything from ghosts to mountains of gold and silver.

However, Joseph's newly found seer stone was nothing compared to an event that occurred when he was 14 years of age. Because in particular the event seemed so similar to his previous treasure hunting, it caused much disbelief and criticism. At a time when religious revivals in the area were causing him mental turmoil 14-year-old Joseph went into the woods to seek guidance from the Lord. As later he would write in his official autobiography:

It was the first time in my life that I had made such an attempt, for amidst all my anxieties I had never as yet made the attempt to pray vocally. . . . I kneeled down and began to offer up the desires of my heart to God. I had scarcely done so, when immediately I was seized upon by some power which entirely overcame me, and had such an astonishing influence over me as to bind my tongue so that I could not speak. Thick darkness gathered around me, and it seemed to me for a time as if I were doomed to sudden destruction. But, exerting all my powers to call upon God to deliver me out of the power of this enemy which had seized upon me, and at the very moment when I was ready to sink into despair and abandon myself to destruction—not to an imaginary ruin, but to the power of some actual being from the unseen world, who had such marvelous power as I had never before felt in any being—just at this moment of great alarm, I saw a pillar of light exactly over my head, above the brightness of the sun, which descended gradually until it fell upon me.

It no sooner appeared than I found myself delivered from the enemy which held me bound. When the light rested upon me I saw two personages, whose brightness and glory defy all description, standing above me in the air. One of them spake unto me, called me by name, and said—pointing to the other—*"This is my beloved Son, hear Him."*

My object in going to inquire of the Lord was to know which of

Joseph Smith.

Hyrum Smith.

93

all the sects was right, that I might know which to join. No sooner, therefore, did I get possession of myself, so as to be able to speak, than I asked the personages who stood above me in the light, which of all the sects was right—and which I should join. I was answered that I must join none of them, for they were all wrong, and the personage who addressed me said that all their creeds were an abomination in His sight; that those professors were all corrupt; that "they draw near to me with their lips, but their hearts are far from me; they teach for doctrines the commandments of men: having a form of godliness, but they deny the power thereof." He again forbade me to join with any of them: and many other things did he say unto me, which I cannot write at this time. When I came to myself again, I found myself lying on my back, looking up into heaven.

Joseph's spirits, in deep despair when he entered the woods, soared as he departed to hurry home. He must first impart the news to his family members, and incredulous though his account was he found the family circle believing rather than scorning him. To them it seemed that the Lord had been training the treasure seeking youth in the proper direction. But the more the story was removed from the family the worse it seemed to be received. A close Methodist minister friend of the family treated the news with contempt, declaring that there was no such thing as vision or revelations in these days, they having ended with the apostles, and that the whole thing was of the devil. The 14-year-old youth who had been a favorite among his neighbors now found himself subject either to humor or scorn. As he would write in his autobiography:

I soon found, however, that my telling the story had excited a great deal of prejudice against me among professors of religion, and was the cause of great persecution, which continued to increase; and though I was an obscure boy, only between fourteen and fifteen years of age, and my circumstances in life such as to make a boy of no consequence in the world, yet men of high standing would take notice sufficient to excite the public mind against me, and create a bitter persecution; and this was common to all the sects—all united to persecute me.

For three years after the event in the woods Joseph waited for but experienced no repeat of the miraculous experience. He prayed often for guidance, hoping for a supernatural follow-up to the miraculous experience that had occurred in the woods. He hoped for this despite the increasing ridicule and scorn as the account of his first experience spread. If he had hoped for otherwise from his story he could see by now that he had more trouble to gain than anything else. Joseph's alternate despair and hope during this probationary period led after three years to the second hallmark experience in his life. As he wrote, it was on the night of September 21, 1823, as he knelt by his bed asking forgiveness for his sins, that a light filled his humble room, a light that made his room lighter than at noonday. Beside him a personage of greater than ordinary stature appeared in the air, standing off the floor. He was clothed in a robe of intense and dazzling whiteness, and in addition his hands, wrists, feet, and ankles as well as his head and neck were bare. To Joseph his countenance truly was like lightning and, in fact, his whole personage was glorious beyond description.

... He called me by name, and said unto me that he was a messenger sent from the presence of God to me and that his name was Moroni; that God had a work for me to do; and that my name should be had for good and evil among all nations, kindreds, and tongues, or that it should be both good and evil spoken of among all people. He said there was a book deposited, written upon gold plates, giving an account of the former inhabitants of this continent, and the sources from whence they sprang. He also said that the fullness of the everlasting Gospel was contained in it, as delivered by the Savior to the ancient inhabitants; also that there were two stones in silver bows—and these stones, fastened to a breastplate, constituted what is called the Urim and Thummin—deposited with the plates; and the possession and use of these stones were what constituted "Seers" in ancient or former times; and that God had prepared them for the purpose of translating the book.

While the angel spoke Joseph was enabled to see a vision of a hillside and in particular the spot upon the hillside where the plates were held in silent trust. Three times that night the angel reappeared to him, and when the heavenly ambassador disappeared for the third time Joseph heard the birds of the air heralding the coming of dawn. That day Joseph went to work in the woods with his father but, feeling faint, started home early. He fell to the ground unconscious, whereupon the angel once more appeared to him and asked him to tell his father what had transpired the night just passed. When he did, his father reassured him that what had happened indeed was truly of God. Now with his father's consent and blessing he went to the hill the angel had shown him, a hill that was higher than any other in that neighborhood, and he at once saw the rounded top of a stone peeping from the ground.

Joseph speedily removed the top soil and found the plates in a stone box along with a sword and breastplate, to which were fastened the supernatural stones Urim and Thummim. The gold plates were about eight inches square and thin. Bound together with three huge rings they were covered with engraved characters. Joseph stretched forth his hands to remove the valuable records, but the messenger forbade him even to touch them until he had become sufficiently instructed in the ways of the kingdom and otherwise purified. Moroni informed him that four years must elapse before he could be permitted to hold and examine the contents of the box, but that meanwhile on each succeeding anniversary of this day he must return to this spot to view the sacred records and be instructed from the Lord and renew his covenants. The angel now imparted many precious truths to Joseph, and he repeated much illumination on each succeeding anniversary visit. Moroni disclosed among other things that he himself was the son of Mormon, a prophet of an ancient people who once had occupied this American land. Joseph opened the box each time, viewed its treasure, replaced the cover, and then covered the box with earth, or did so until the year of his last such visit in 1827.

It was earlier in this year of 1827 that another hallmark event occurred in Joseph's life. He was married, and his marriage, too, had involved the supernatural. Joseph's fame was continuing to spread so much that from a distant part of the state a farmer came visiting the Smiths' home at Palmyra, New York. He had heard of Joseph's clairvoyant ability, and when Joseph without difficulty described the visiting farmer's distant farmhouse and other buildings, he was hired at once to assist in helping look for a lost silver mine in a vicinity known by the farmer. The search for the mine proved fruitless, but it was on that trip that Joseph met and on January 18, 1827, married dark-complexioned and attractive Emma Hale from Harmony, Vermont. And it was on September 22, 1827, after the couple

96

had returned to Joseph's home in Palmyra, that Joseph visited his hidden treasure on the hill for the fifth and last time. In this instance the angel Moroni permitted him to take the treasure from the stone box home with him.

With the golden book in his hand Joseph found that it was about six inches in thickness. Though a part of the volume was sealed he was able to turn the other pages with his fingers and saw that they were covered on both sides with strange characters, small and beautifully engraved. Moroni instructed Joseph to make no attempt to open the sealed part of the book because that time was not yet here. He advised him to shield the entire volume from profane touch and sight, even with his life. Moroni also told him that efforts would be made to rob him of the holy writings, but if he proved faithful he would triumph. With a parting promise that after Joseph completed the labor of translating the plates Moroni would return for them, Moroni disappeared. So now, with the plates hidden under his mantle and with the Urim and Thummim stones to serve as seer stones to help with the translation, and also carrying the breastplate, Joseph sped homeward. And even enroute homeward Moroni's prophecy began unfolding at once. Three times during his brief journey homeward Joseph was attacked by unknown assailants. But the young man, more than six feet tall and powerful, fought them off and arrived home breathless though safe.

Even though his large family stuck with him throughout, with the possible exception of a cynical younger brother, as they had since his first historic supernatural experience at age fourteen, what happened to Joseph after he brought home the treasure has historical parallel only perhaps in the persecuted life of Christ. As word spread of the supernatural event when Joseph was fourteen, and then three years later the discovery of the treasure, and then four years after that his bringing it home, scorn in many areas began to turn either to greed or hate. Only gradually did a few non-family members become believers and then disciples.

As word continued to spread, the best thing that most people could think to say about that young upstart Joseph Smith was that either he was a joke or a hoax, his latter intention most likely being to sell interest in his treasure. Making this aspect more probable was his continuing claim that he had orders from heaven that no one but he be allowed to see the treasure. Even at nis own home he thus either had to keep his treasure hidden in a box or covered with a cloth or otherwise out of view. Worse than buying a pig in a poke, people might be asked to purchase treasure in a box. Among the worst that could be said about him was that he was an imposter, claiming like Christ to have special instructions from heaven to establish a new kingdom upon earth. What hit hard here, as in the time of Christ, was that his mission met head on with already established religion. And too, as with Christ, people began to worry that his mission was to replace the political status quo as well. Like Christ, the religion he preached was of a God active in the lives of mankind. As Joseph the Prophet himself exemplified time and again throughout his adult life, and as Christ predicted, a God active in human life can lead to healing of afflictions, prophecy, clairvoyance, and countless other miracles.

In her biography of Joseph and other family members published 26 years later, Joseph's mother Lucy would write about those strange treasures brought into her household that day of September 22, 1827. She would explain that Joseph always kept hidden two of the three categories of treasures. He would show only the pair of treasure stones, the Urim and the Thummim, which she described as magic spectacles consisting of "two smooth three-cornered diamonds set in glass and the glasses set in silver bows." But as for the breastplate, this he kept wrapped in a handkerchief. "It was concave on one side and convex on the other, and extended from the neck downwards as far as the center of a man of extraordinary size." She could not even discern this much of the golden plates, for Joseph warned his family as well as all others that it meant instant death if they were looked upon by other than he. He changed the book's hiding places often in his house and elsewhere, and on one occasion left an empty box as a decoy in a neighbor's shop. When the shop was raided the empty box was all the neighbors found.

Being plagued by questions from his own family as well as actual searches by others, Joseph found it impossible in his father's home to write the book's translation. A neighbor, Martin Harris, agreed to finance the move of Joseph and his wife Emma to her home town of Harmony, Pennsylvania, and to follow later and help translate by serving as a secretary. So Joseph and Emma moved to a house in Harmony furnished them by her father, this despite the fact that her father was greatly and often annoyed when Joseph showed him only a box but never even a peek inside at what were purported to be some fabled golden plates in the form of a book. Time and again he refused his father-in-law's request to inspect the contents.

Emma was Joseph's first scribe to write down the plates' translation, although she never saw the plates even though they often lay wrapped in a small linen tablecloth on the table. Only when she moved the plates to dust the table did her fingers ever feel them under their covering. Then and later she described them as feeling like sheets of thick paper and sounding like metal when the bundle was moved. As she took down his dictation she was most mystified by the fact that her husband either by staring into his Urim and Thummim or at other times by staring into his small seer stone from the well could translate the plates' characters with the plates still wrapped. Joseph explained that what he was translating was a history of the Indians from the earliest times, and as he translated, it became clear that what he was translating was in many ways similar in format and style to the King James Bible. He discovered that as he translated Indian historical lore, among other things the book solved the long-debated question of the history of the red man's origin on American soil.

The neighbor, Harris, who had financed the move of Joseph and Emma from Palmyra to Harmony had a wife who throughout thought him a fool. She nagged him continually about his crazy financial backing of what she called the Golden Book. Thus prodded, Martin came to Harmony and asked for visual proof by means of his personal sight of the plates. Though Joseph on various occasions did permit Harris to lift the clapboard chest containing the plates, enabling Harris to estimate their weight at 40 to 50 pounds, Joseph remained unyielding in refusing to display the contents. Harris pressed a demand at least to see a copy of the engraved characters and to take them to New York City to see if learned men there could throw any light on them. When Joseph explained that the characters were "reformed Egyptian," Harris entreated that he be allowed to take whatever they were to New York for identification. Joseph at last agreed, and Harris carried a copy of the characters to an eminent professor of Greek and Latin at Columbia College in New York City. The professor put in writing that the copy "consisted of all kinds of crooked characters disposed in columns, and had evidently been prepared by some person who had before him at the time a book containing various alphabets. Greek and Hebrew letters, crosses and flourishes, Roman letters inverted or placed sideways, were. . .copied in such a way as not to betray the source whence it was derived." Though Harris was altogether convinced and returned home dedicated to the idea of risking his $10,000 farm in financing the Book of Mormon, the Columbia professor later repudiated his written statement. After learning about the story of the angel and the golden plates and about the unlearned country author who reportedly could not write, and at best had only a few years formal education, the professor tore up his statement and stormed, "I cannot read a sealed book."

However, Harris in his new dedication took over where Emma had left off and began to write down the story of the Book of Mormon. Though Joseph and Harris worked in the same room a blanket flung across a rope separated them. On one side Joseph sat staring into his stones, and on the other Harris sat writing at a table. Harris adhered to Joseph's warning that God would fell him if he even looked at the plates while they were being translated, but on one occasion Harris did test Joseph by substituting an ordinary stone for the seer stone, a test Joseph passed.

They worked together two months, laboriously, a process more difficult because of Joseph's own lack of writing ability. The two months' work, plus what Emma had written down previously, produced only 116 pages of foolscap. Because Harris believed Joseph's translation to be the inspired word of God, he changed nothing. The result was a manuscript with hardly a capital letter, comma, or period in any of it—in other words a manuscript with almost no punctuation. With the future publication of the Book of Mormon, the typesetters broke up the sentences almost as they saw fit.

Meanwhile Harris begged Joseph to be allowed to take these first 116 pages of the manuscript home to show his wife, and with great reluctance Joseph at last gave in to his financial backer's insistence. The result was catastrophic. Harris's wife, furious at his continued financial backing of the so-called Golden Book, stole the manuscript, hid it, and neither blessings nor blows could force her to reveal its whereabouts. Because the manuscript never was found, it seemed probable she destroyed it. Joseph spent weeks in turmoil. Lost was the written translation of a thousand years of mainly political Indian history. At last he looked into his Urim and Thummim and prayed for a revelation. It came. He would translate other parts of the golden plates. This next translation would emphasize the religious rather than the political history of the lost 116 pages. Thus the theft of Joseph's first 116 pages of translation, though causing him at the time great trial, proved yet another hallmark.

Joseph's Book of Mormon that came out of this second period of translation became one of the most famous religious works in world history. Martin Harris had proved himself unreliable, but now came an early important convert who had heard of and believed in Joseph and his mission and who now arrived at Joseph's home. Ardently offering his services, this young former school teacher began taking dictation at once. Compared to the previous laborious pace, the pace of this second manuscript was phenomenal. They began working together on April 7, 1829, and by the first week in July had completed a 275,000-word manuscript. A tenth of this Book of Mormon consisted of direct quotations from the Bible, but the remaining nine-tenths were elaborations, analyses, and conclusions, including long sermons and profound theological arguments.

One day in the spring of 1829, just before completion of the book, Joseph and his school teacher scribe went for a prayerful walk in the woods, and John the Baptist appeared to them. After this, miracles seemed to spread wherever the word of Mormon went. Now Joseph showed the golden plates to others. Three witnesses, including the scribe school teacher, signed a statement drawn up by Joseph witnessing their viewing of the plates. Entitled "The Testimony Of Three Witnesses," the approximately 200-word statement described in detail the plates as Joseph himself earlier had described them. And then he showed the plates to eight other men, and they, too, signed generally similar statements. A number of these witnesses and later his wife Emma emphasized the size, weight, and metallic texture of the plates.

Martin Harris mortgaged his farm for $3,000 to pay for the printing of 5,000 copes of the Book of Mormon based upon the translation from the plates, and by March 26, 1830, the first copies of the Book of Mormon went on sale in the Palmyra bookstore. Within a few days after publication of the Book of Mormon, Joseph, on Tuesday, April 6, 1830, with six members, formally established his Church of Christ, which he described as the restored religion of Jesus Himself. Within a month the number had jumped to 40.

The growth of the Church of Jesus Christ of Latter-Day Saints from those early 40 members to its present worldwide membership of more than three million is the most spectacular religious phenomenon in United States history. The church grew despite or perhaps because of early severe persecutions. The first published review of the *Book of Mormon* was itself an ominous portent of the criticism, persecution, and death that would haunt early believers in Joseph the Prophet and his book.

Mormons persecuted by non-Mormons for 24 years were forced to zig-zag across thousands of miles of American territory. They trekked from New York to Ohio, Missouri, Illinois, and, finally, across the Great Plains and the Rocky Mountains to their modern headquarters in Salt Lake City, Utah. They suffered from their inability to put on public view the famous golden plates witnessed only by about a dozen before Heaven reclaimed the plates. The Mormons did such odd things as perform healings, make prophecies, and talk in tongues. Their formal religious structure, too, was much different from that of their neighbors. They built impressive two and three-story temple structures rather than less pretentious churches. Every church member had a specific church duty and title, from that of the president, Joseph the Prophet, on down next to 12 disciples, then to a council of 70, and down through the hierarchy. They based every important decision upon divine revelation received almost entirely by Joseph Smith alone.

In material terms the Mormons, when left alone, most often prospered and built large stores, mills, barns, storehouses, schools, and homes, in general evincing a prosperous communal life in which all were to work for the common good. Their charismatic young leader had a handsome, commanding appearance, asked for and received the military title of lieutenant-general, ran on the Mormon ticket for office of the president of the United States, and let it be known widely that because of inadequate national and state protection the Mormons could afford their own protection of tightly organized Mormon militia. Surrounding the organized Mormons came more and more individualistic frontiersmen, uneducated, many times unlawful, and in fact often an unruly mob that looked with envy upon the prosperous Mormon holdings. Joining with these were the staunch church folk of traditional religious beliefs.

Joseph Smith ran a tight organization, but its rapid growth made it large enough that he had defections. The final stop of the Mormon pilgrimage east of the Mississippi was Nauvou, Illinois, a former malaria-infected swampland that the enterprising Mormons had made into a prosperous frontier town. It and the countryside harbored about 16,000 Mormons. When Prophet Smith had a revelation that he should establish polygamy, and set an example by taking unto himself perhaps as many as 50 wives or more, some otherwise single and some otherwise married, he found himself facing his most serious internal Mormon dissent. In fact, the downfall of Joseph and his brother Hyrum was the direct result of allegations, true or false, that Joseph asked the wife of one of his leading church members to join him as one of his own heavenly wives. In anger her husband took his wife away, established a nearby newspaper, and when its attack became too scurrilous Joseph had his Mormon Legion march to the newspaper office, wreck the press, and burn every newspaper they could find. Hoping to spare Nauvou's destruction Joseph and his brother Hyrum and some other leading Mormons turned themselves over to non-Mormon militia, although Joseph himself had a strong prescience of death for himself and his brother. The militia placed the Mormons in jail at Carthage, Illinois, and on June 27, 1844, a mob stormed the jail and Joseph and his brother died in the barrage of bullets. As the one-time beautiful and prosperous city of Nauvou was being sacked behind them, one of the late-Prophet's 12 disciples, Brigham Young, led most of the Mormons to relative safety across the wilderness of the plains and the Rocky Mountain to their future headquarters of Salt Lake City.

It has been said that few people ever lived who deserved more to find a golden book and lead a persecuted people out of one danger and out of another than Joseph the Prophet. Not because of ascetic qualification. Far from it. The robust, hard living, virile amateur body wrestler much preferred silk shirts to hair shirts. What qualified Joseph the Prophet was that his colorful and charismatic leadership could convince millions of people, from closest friends and relatives to strangers across wide oceans, that when he proffered his golden book followed by other divine revelations from God almost daily for more than a decade, they had better believe it. (The most authoritative work about the life of Joseph Smith is in *History of the Church of Jesus Christ of Latter-Day Saints. Period I. History of Joseph Smith, the Prophet, by Himself.* 6 vols., Mormon Church, Salt Lake City, Utah. A scholarly and thorough though skeptical work is *No Man Knows My History, The Life of Joseph Smith*, Fawn M. Brodie, Alfred A. Knopf, 1971. The author took her main title from a sermon to an audience of 10,000 that Joseph Smith preached to in Nauvou, Illinois, two months before his murder: "You don't know me; you never knew my heart. No man knows my history. I cannot tell it; I shall never understand it. I don't blame anyone for not believing my history. If I had not experienced what I have, I could not have believed it myself.")

Proving That Matter
Is An Illusion

MARY BAKER EDDY (A.D. July 16, 1821-December 3, 1910). U.S.A. New Hampshire. Bow.

Youngest of a family of three sons and three daughters, Mary was born to Mark and Abigail Baker in the village of Bow. The Bakers were a prosperous farming family, and father Mark Baker was a community, civic, and religious leader. A deacon in the local Congregational Church, he and his devout wife Abigail took the family every Sunday to morning and evening services, and each day during the week the family knelt together for morning and evening prayer services at home.

Mary was a pretty girl, bright, with a sense of humor, and the other children and her parents tended to pamper this youngest family member, if pampering could be said possible in the strict family life of that day. She enjoyed reading, writing, and memorization, including many hours of reading and memorizing the Bible and writing poems and essays on religious themes. Her father's favorite, strong-willed like him, she came to savor and practice forceful theological discussions, as did he. But unlike her frugal father, she was considered most generous of all family members, possibly excepting her mother, and had to be cautioned on various occasions about giving her things to needy children at school.

At age eight Mary had an unusual experience involving her generous and devout mother. One day Mary thought she heard her mother calling her. Mary answered, only to have her mother tell her that she had not called her to start with. "But, Mother, who did call me?" Mary insisted. "I heard someone call 'Mary' three times." This incident repeated itself a number of times, and eventually Mary did not bother to answer nor to ask of her mother if she had called. Then one day a 15-year-old girl cousin visited and was sitting with Mary when the voice came again. The cousin looked at Mary, expecting her to answer, and then finally said sharply, "Mary, your mother is calling you." Mary sought her mother, but as on those other occasions her mother said she had not called. After Mary explained that her cousin also had heard the voice, her mother questioned the cousin firmly and was told with equal firmness that the cousin indeed had heard the voice.

That night, after the latest episode, Mary's mother tucked her youngest daughter into bed and read her the story of Samuel from the Bible. The mother, "a sainted mother in all walks of life" as described by her youngest daughter, told Mary that if the voice came to her again she was to answer in the words of Samuel: "Speak, Lord; for thy servant heareth." Later the voice did come again, but this time Mary was too afraid to answer. Afterwards she cried and prayed for forgiveness and promised the next time to follow her mother's bidding. When the call re-occurred, Mary was obedient and answered, "Speak, Lord, for thy servant heareth." Never did the call come again.

At the age of 12 Mary, the only one of the Baker children to do so, made a public profession of faith during a protracted revival meeting at the nearby First Congregational Church in Concord. In 1837 the Baker family moved to a farm near near-by Sanbornton, and there Mary's parents and she now at age 17 publicly joined the Congregational Church. But the hearing of the voice and then the public profession of faith followed by her joining of the church seem to have been spiritual highlights in an otherwise increasingly tragic first 45 years for Mary Baker. Frail from childhood on, succumbing to first one physical sickness and then another, she spent her adult life to age 45 more and more bedridden. Yet among a great number of her family members and friends she physically was the lucky one. She was very closely attached to her brother Albert, a rising young attorney and a member of the New Hampshire legislature. Albert was a political protege of Gen. Franklin Pierce, who was himself on the way to the presidency of the United States. Shortly after

106

Mary's close friend's father died, tragedy struck again. Seemingly on the threshhold of an illustrious career, Albert died at age 31. Thus the youngest member of the grief-stricken Baker family found herself early in life experiencing afflictions and tragedy beyond her years.

Two years and two months after the death of her brother, Mary, in December 1843, recovered enough from despair and illnesses to marry a tall, handsome, and already successful young businessman named George Washington Glover. But in North Carolina her husband was stricken with fever and nine days later died, after only six months of marriage. Fourteen hundred miles from home, pregnant, frail, with a lifetime history of chronic illnesses on some occasions almost fatal, Mary undertook the grueling journey homeward, changing from steamboat to ferryboat to railroad cars and seemingly repeating the cycle many times. Her health deteriorated rapidly after the journey, though her son was born safely. Too frail to care for her son, the afflicted mother required help from relatives and other friends. In 1953, nine years after the death of her husband, a local dentist, Dr. Daniel Patterson, indicated a desire to marry the semi-invalid Mrs. Glover and to help rear her son. But after marriage the dentist not only refused to permit his sickly wife to bring her son into his home, he became shiftless and nonproductive, avoiding bankruptcy by borrowing money from one of Mary's sisters.

Meanwhile, Mary continued to pray and read the Bible and any other religious book she could get her hands on. Children in the neighborhood nicknamed her "the good sick lady." One day a mother and her baby stopped by to see her. The baby's eyes were seriously inflamed, but Mary, known for her love of children, took the baby in her arms and remembered Jesus' words, "Suffer the little children to come unto me and forbid them not." When she handed the baby back to the mother the mother exclaimed that the child's eyes were perfectly clear and could see.

Mary's father died. And in this same unpleasant era Mary's dentist husband began leaving his sickly wife on more and more occasions, taking longer and longer trips ostensibly to look for dentistry patients. During one of his absences Mary ventured outside on the ice and fell. She was carried unconscious into a

Mary Baker Eddy's health was restored instantly when she was 45, and from that time onward there developed one of the world's best known supernatural concepts, "the power of mind over matter."

nearby house, and the doctor arrived and said that she was suffering from grave head injuries and that there appeared to be a spinal dislocation. She was wrapped in fur robes and taken home where her friends began gathering, as it seemed that she might not recover. The minister was called and came quickly. On Sunday morning on his way to church he stopped again, and after he and Mrs. Patterson prayed together, she asked him to come again after the service: The minister replied by asking her if she knew the critical nature of her injury and that she was sinking and might not survive through the day. She assured the minister that she was aware of all this, but that she had such faith in God that she felt He would raise her up. The minister departed and some other friends dropped by and told her they would return that evening. Mary answered, "When you come the next time, I will be sitting up in the next room."

Mary Baker's friends wondered if she might not be delirious. But she asked now to be alone, to read the Bible, and pray. She read the ninth chapter of the New Testament of the Bible about Jesus' healing of the man who was paralyzed. As she read, a sense of peace came to her. Abruptly the full assurance of God's presence flooded her being with light. Revealed was a divine view of the things she had hungered and thirsted for through the years. If God was anything, He was everything. If he was spirit, then everything was spirit. If He was love, then everything was love. If He was whole, then everything was whole. Any suggestion to the contrary was a dream, an illusion.

Mary realized that she was well. Her health returned instantly. She went joyously to tell her friends. The year was 1866, and she was 45. For the next 44 years, until her death in 1910, she healed others and instructed others how to heal, wrote periodicals and books, and formed the famed Mother Church, the First Church of Christ Scientist in Boston, Massachusetts. Other branches formed as this religious phenomenon spread in a manner unparalleled in western annals since the birth of Christ.

Mary Patterson's new-found faith widened the gulf even more between her and her dentist husband. Her husband deserted her yet another time, this time for good; and after more than seven years of this last separation, they divorced. She changed her name back to Mary Baker Glover, in memory of

Mary Baker Eddy seemed as venerable as the church she founded.

her lovable husband and that young marriage that had ended so tragically. Eventually, in 1877, she married a devoted Christian Scientist and worker whom she had healed, Asa Gilbert Eddy. He was an active Christian Science teacher during the five years of their marriage until he died, and she retained the name Mary Baker Eddy.

The best known book produced in the Christian Science movement is Mrs. Eddy's *Science And Health With A Key To The Scriptures.* Among many other publications out of Mrs. Eddy's church has come *The Christian Science Monitor,* an internationally respected newspaper. (An interesting account of the life of Mary Baker Eddy, clearly written for young people as well as adults, is in *Mary Baker Eddy: The Golden Days,* Jewel Spangler Smaus, The Christian Science Publishing Society, 1966.)

The Mother Church soon became a Boston landmark.

Raising Oneself
From The Dead

JESUS CHRIST (circa 7 B.C.-A.D. 26). Galilee. Nazareth.

He was born to devout Jewish parents Joseph and Mary, in direct line of descent from King David through Joseph, influence of the Holy Spirit on Mary permitting immaculate conception without a human father. Jewish shepherds and Persian Magi came to herald the birth of the child in a manger in Bethlehem. His parents named him Jesus (Greek form of the Hebrew word Joshua or Aramaic form of the word Yeshua).

The child grew up in Nazareth not far from an international highway along which passed many merchants and soldiers. Once the youth visited Jerusalem with his parents and astounded hearers by the calibre of questions he asked teachers there. Modern scholarship indicates that Joseph must have died in Jesus' early manhood and that the young man fell heir to running the carpenter's business and caring for the remainder of the family, four boys and at least two girls.

When Jesus was about 30, an ascetic named John the Baptist appeared in Galilee, announcing the coming of the Messiah whom so many Jews expected. John baptized many people in the river Jordan, and Jesus also went to him to be baptized. Spiritual illumination at the time of Jesus' baptism, exhibited physically by the appearance of a dove, marked the beginning of Jesus' three-year span of public ministry on earth. After the baptism he sojourned in the desert beyond Jordan to ponder his rapidly unfolding divine role.

Herod Antipas, ruler of Galilee, later imprisoned and murdered John. It was after this when Jesus returned from the desert and began to teach in the coastal towns along the sea of Galilee. Quickly he became popular among all classes of people. He worked with outcast and depressed classes, but Roman centurians also came to him for help. He was described as a "friend of sinners" and accused of "eating with publicans and sinners," but eventually these descriptions became descriptions of reverence. Among 12 disciples who joined him and others who were converted by him were uneducated fishermen but also scholars and civil leaders. The teachings of Jesus in the form of parables was popularly accepted, and today they are considered one of the most attractive portions of the Christian Bible.

Jesus' ministry, based on the doctrine that God is love and that in the kingdom of God there can be no disease, strongly emphasized healing. He healed the sick, caused the lame to walk, the blind to see, and raised people from the dead. In addition to healings he fed a multitude from a few loaves and fishes, walked on water, and transported himself great distances instantly, showing that all things are possible to those who believe. His fame spread far beyond his physical presence. Large numbers of people began calling him Christ (Greek version of Jewish word Messiah) as his teachings spread into Gentile areas and became a world religion. Jesus regarded himself as the manifestation of God on earth, and his disciples and other followers not only called him Christ but also Son of God.

After spending his two or three years of public ministry along the northern coastal towns of the sea of Galilee and neighboring districts, including perhaps occasional visits to Jerusalem, Jesus made a triumphant though final entry into the holy city. Symbolically he entered Jerusalem on a beast of burden, as had been prophesied by the prophet Zechariah, rather than on a horse as a victorious Christ or Messiah. His coming and heretic teaching in the temple courts were resented by the Sadducee priests. Jesus on the Mount of Olives in the Garden of Gethsemane told his disciples that the end was at hand, prophesying that one of his disciples, Judas, would betray him. The Sadducee priests seized Jesus by night, a hastily summoned Jewish court tried him for heresy, and then in front

Christ was baptized in this Jordan River.

of the Roman governor Pilate accused him of high treason. His teachings always had emphasized forgiveness of enemies, "turning the other cheek," and he did not now defend himself. Herod refused to try Jesus, but Pilate yielded, apparently because of fear of public revolt. On a skull-shaped hill called Golgotha or Calvary they nailed Jesus to a cross between two thieves. In mockery they put a crown of thorns on his head, a spear in his side, and gave him vinegar when he asked for water. But Jesus prayed aloud, "Father, forgive them for they know not what they do." In a moment of desperation Jesus cried out also, "My God, why hast thou forsaken me?" It was a quotation from Psalm 22 of the Old Testament of the Bible, a psalm of suffering but ending with hope. At the moment of Jesus' death on Friday the sky darkened, and a cloth was rent in the temple. That same day Jesus was put in a tomb, and there was physical desertion and doubt among his disciples as well as among the multitudes. If Jesus had indeed been the Messiah, why couldn't he have saved himself?

However, sight of a resurrected Jesus dissipated fears and changed despair into triumph. The New Testament records five accounts of the resurrection appearance of Jesus, all five in different style and emphasis but similar in substance, as five different people differently report the same actual historic event. In addition to appearances to relatives and close disciples Jesus appeared to 500 other disciples before visibly ascending into heaven. In addition to his early and tragic death, unlike typically great spiritual leaders, he performed the recorded feat before hundreds of witnesses of having raised himself from the dead. He became the subject of the most comprehensive and analytical literature in recorded history. In A.D. 354 the Bishop of Rome established December 25 as the most likely date for the birth of Christ, and Christmas on this date has become a historic celebration in large areas throughout the world.

Reading A Book Or A Body Without Opening Either

**EDGAR CAYCE (A.D. March 18, 1887-January 3, 1945).
U.S.A. Kentucky. Hopkinsville.**

Of five children born to Carrie Major and Leslie B. Cayce (pronounced Casey), Edgar was the oldest and only son. The Cayces were devout worshippers at the local Christian Church, an offshoot of the Presbyterian. The father, Leslie Cayce, known as "the Squire" because of his regal manner, had been forced to support the family first as a farmer, then part-time magistrate, and finally as storekeeper. Though the Squire's father, Edgar's grandfather Thomas Cayce, was a locally well-known psychic who easily divined water throughout southwestern Kentucky, such psychic ability apparently bypassed the Squire. Instead, as happens so often, it skipped a full generation, moving from the grandfather to reappear again in the grandson Edgar. Edgar's extremely devout mother also exhibited strong clairvoyant traits, especially relating with her son.

The first of many supernatural landmarks in Edgar's life came at age four, at the time of his grandfather's death. Edgar was riding on his grandfather's lap when the horse stumbled into a pond. His grandfather threw Edgar clear but lost his own life, Edgar watching terrified as the horse in its panic trampled his grandfather to death. From his grandfather's funeral Edgar slipped away to an area under the limbs of the maple trees in back of his father's farmhouse. There he began conversing with some boys and girls who had appeared. Edgar's father came to him, perplexed, chiding Edgar for talking to himself. When Ed-

116

gar turned to point out his new-found friends, they had disappeared, returning only after his father's departure. In describing the event the unbelieving father had said, "That boy is like an old man. Not only is he solemn, but he's forever seeing things that aren't there." The Squire had occasion to make this observation a number of times later, as Edgar from time to time discoursed with strange companions seen only to Edgar himself. The youth's unseen guests also caused occasional banter from Edgar's younger sisters, but he took the banter as good-natured repartee among a family that seemed closely devoted to each other.

At age 10 Edgar started reading the Bible every day. To this end he went into the woods beyond his family's farm, built a small lean-to out of timber and foliage, and dug a drinking-water well for himself, perhaps as his grandfather would have done. At this site, curled up on the ground with leaves for a bed and pillow, he formed a lasting love for Bible reading. Replacing his companions from his grandfather's funeral now came a personification of various characters in a setting out of the Bible itself: Noah and the Ark, Joseph and his coat of many colors, Lot's wife turned to a pillar of salt, Daniel in the lion's den, David and his slingshot with which he slew the giant Goliath, and of course Jesus healing the afflicted including the raising of others and himself from the dead.

Edgar read his Bible every day for three straight years, until he was 13. Then one evening at dusk he looked up and saw a woman standing before him. She was a stranger, though in age and build she somewhat resembled his mother. The strange woman spoke gently. "Your prayers have been answered. Say what it is you want most, so that I may give it to you." When he recovered enough to speak, he heard himself saying, "I would like to be helpful to other people, especially children when they are sick."

The visitor gave off such a brilliant hue Edgar momentarily turned his head, for relief, but when he returned to face her again she was gone. Disturbed, he found himself wondering if he had been dreaming or if she had been real.

Still distraught, Edgar ran home and told his mother of the lady's visit and her promise. "Do you think I have been reading the Bible too much?" he asked his mother. His mother took the

Edgar Cayce.

Bible from his hands and softly read to him from the Gospel of St. John. "Verily, verily, I say unto you. Whatsoever ye shall ask the father in my name, he will give it to you. Hitherto have ye asked nothing in my name; ask, and ye shall receive, that your joy may be full." His mother added to her son, "You have always wanted to help others, and this may be what the lady of the vision meant by your prayers having been heard."

After his meeting with the stranger, Edgar Cayce's life became one of the strangest on record, not only in the annals of Kentucky but in the history of the world. Considered a dullard in school, the daydreaming youth was still in the third grade at age 12. But after the visit from the lady he could curl up in a chair with his head resting on a pillow and a book under it, and when he awoke about five minutes later could recite every word between the hardcovers. With a spelling book, for example, he not only could spell every word in the book, over which his head had rested, he could tell an inquirer which words were next to the word the inquirer had asked to be spelled.

Edgar Cayce's knowledge of the Bible plus his spiritual fervor enabled him to become an outstanding Sunday School teacher at his church. Another highlight of his religious life oc-

Under the title of Association For Research And Enlightenment, the Edgar Cayce Foundation carries on its founder's work at Virginia Beach, Virginia.

curred one day during a walk in the Kentucky woods when by a mysterious encounter he conversed with Dwight L. Moody, a famed evangelist visiting in Hopkinsville. This was years before the evangelist established the Moody Bible Institute in Chicago, outside which passers-by were said to have been "felled by the spirit" simply from walking along the sidewalk outside Moody's office.

However, it was Cayce's healing ability which gave him his place in history and led to the foundation of the Association for Research and Enlightenment, increasingly active today from Virginia Beach, Virginia, U.S.A. In diagnosing and healing, his usual procedure was to loosen his tie, take off his shoes, lie down, and almost immediately enter a trance. Then in response to questioning from an interrogator in his presence as he himself slept, he accurately would diagnose an illness and prescribe proper treatment for patients, often many miles distant. In addition to his numerous recorded healings of the afflicted, including more than 14,000 documented stenographic records of his telepathic-clairvoyant readings over the years, he is on record as foreseeing many future events. He saw his future wife in a vision and met her physically exactly as he had foreseen her, and they were married. They left Hopkinsville in 1912, and with their son Hugh Lynn Cayce, who now heads the organizational portion of his father's program, lived in various areas that included Anniston, Alabama; Selma, Alabama; parts of Texas; Dayton, Ohio; and then a permanent residence at Virginia Beach, Virginia. Sceptics have attempted to disprove the powers of Edgar Cayce, including one occasion when a team of several doctors stuck various kinds of sharp objects into him to test the validity of his trance. Yet almost four decades after the death of Edgar and his wife Gertrude in 1945, many thousands of students worldwide gather in organized groups to study the essence of what Edgar Cayce taught and did. (For a firsthand account of Edgar Cayce, by a trained social scientist who personally heard Cayce give more than 500 "readings," see *Edgar Cayce On Religion And Experience*, Harmon H. Bro, Association For Research And Enlightenment, 1970. And for a fascinating coverage of Edgar Cayce in his formative years see *A Prophet In His Own Country*, Jess Stearn, William Morrow and Company, 1974.)

Reading Even Though Illiterate

MUHAMMAD (A.D. 570-632). Arabia. Mecca.

Muhammad (servant of Allah) was born into the ruling Quraysh (Koreish) tribe in Mecca. As he matured he accompanied trading caravans between Mecca and Syria, and en route participated in defensive battles against would-be marauders. A rich widow named Khadija, about 40 years of age, had hired Muhammad to work for her, and when he himself was age 25 the two married. Khadija greatly influenced Muhammad, especially in his early religious experiences, and as long as she lived she was his only wife and bore him seven children.

When about 40 years of age Muhammad began having unusual dreams and visions. During the month of Ramadan he sojourned in the mountains and there discovered that even bushes and rocks saluted him. Then a startling figure, calling himself the archangel Gabriel, appeared and hailed Muhammad as the Apostle of God, after which he reappeared with writing for Muhammad to read. Though Muhammad was illiterate, because the written words were the words of God Muhammad unhesitantly read the words that form the ninety-sixth chapter of the Koran: "Recite, in the name of the Lord who created, Created man from clotted blood." Muhammad was so distraught by what he had witnessed that he returned to seek comfort from his wife Khadija. Her husband was a prophet, she realized, the first so to perceive him.

Though the spiritual revelations ceased for a while, they

121

reappeared even more strongly, and Muhammad began calling people from their worship of idols. He preached a simple message, "There is no god but Allah," and insisted that all other gods of Mecca were false, and must be destroyed. Muhammad's first male convert was his boy cousin Ali, later a caliph, a title taken by Muhammad's successors as heads of Islam. Muhammad, now being persecuted by the rulers of Quraysh because of his attack on their idols, decided in A.D. 622 to move to Medina with his Meccan followers. This migration (Hijra or Hegira) has henceforth been commemorated as the beginning of the era of the Muslim or Moslem, the Islamic name for true believer. The Muslim calendar dates from this A.D. 622. Muhammad died ten years later, in 632, and his tomb in Medina attracts many thousands of followers annually. His succeeding caliph in the Islamic movement assured the faithful that Muhammad had been only a man and mortal, and that instead of worshipping him they must worship only God.

Despite the various challenges to Islam the Quran, in former times spelled Koran or Alcoran, has been a strikingly unifying book strongly revered by millions of Muslims. These faithful believe that the Quran is the uncreated word of God, originating with the "Mother of the Book" maintained in the presence of God and sent down by the angel Gabriel as the Quran to Muhammad on the "night of power." However backward its leaders sometimes may appear, Muhammad established a missionary religion similar to that of Hinduism, Buddhism, and Christianity. So in various areas, especially Africa, Muhammad's religion of Islam is winning converts to the idea of one God and one spiritual peer, or Muhammad.

Muhammad established a missionary religion that has led to more and more mosques such as these for an increasing number of followers worldwide.

Reversing The Law
Of Gravity

TERESA (A.D. March 28, 1515-October 4, 1582). Spain. Old Castile. Avila.

Teresa was born into a substantial family, substantial in terms of number as well as community ranking. She was one of two daughters among nine children born to Alphonsus Sanchez and Beatrice Ahumada. Earlier Alphonsus Sanchez had three children by a first wife, making Teresa one of a household of 12 children. It was a learned and pious Catholic household. The family was known for its charity to the poor, compassion for the sick, and tenderness toward the servants. The well-used library was stocked with good books. Alphonsus was known for his purity and aversion to swearing. Also very virtuous was Teresa's mother Beatrice, who suffered from frequent sickness and died at age 33 when Teresa was 12.

From her earliest years Teresa showed a strong allegiance to pious living. By age seven she became engrossed in reading works on the lives of the saints and other pious books, and soon a younger brother was sharing with her this enjoyment. The lives of Christian martyrs so fascinated the young sister and brother they ran away from home to head for the land of the Moors, telling each other they were hoping to die for their faith. As they went they continued to pray that God would keep them inspired with his holy love so that they might lay down their lives for Christ. But their fervent pilgrimage proved short-lived. Not far outside town at a bridge an uncle intercepted and hustled them back to an irritated family in general and a distraught mother in particular. Though the brother laid all the blame on his older sister, both were chastised. Undaunted, the two next decided to become hermits at home and constructed in the family garden miniature hermitages made of piles of stones. Meanwhile Teresa continued her own devout private devotions. She said long prayers, especially the Rosary. In her room she had a picture of Christ with the Samaritan woman at the well, and often she would look at that picture and pray earnestly to Christ, "Lord, give me of that water," meaning that she prayed for Christ's grace and love.

When Teresa was 12 her mother died, and the grief-stricken child fell to her knees before a picture of the Virgin Mary and begged through her tears that the Virgin Mary would herself replace her dead mother. Teresa credited this childlike act with bringing great reward to her throughout the remainder of her life, the Virgin Mary seeming thereafter to respond to all requests from Teresa.

Teresa was an intelligent, pretty, popular child. For a few months in her early teens her religious ardor seemed to lessen as she began concentrating upon "fine clothes and perfumes" and reading romances which were frowned upon by the Catholic family and church. Her father decided to remove her from these distractions by placing her in a convent where many of the higher class young ladies of their hometown of Avila were educated. After about a week in the convent, Teresa began forgetting the worldly distractions and fell more and more into convent life. Still, however, she lacked the courage and desire to become a full-fledged nun.

After a year and a half in the convent, Teresa fell dangerously ill and her father brought her home. As she recovered she spent many happy hours discussing religion with close relatives, including an older sister and a pious uncle. Her health in general was bad, and after recovering from the first illness she again fell ill, this time with a violent fever. She read more religious writings and spent longer periods in earnest prayer, and with this she found herself determined to become a nun. Surprisingly, perhaps, her father now said that he felt that this was going too far and that he would refuse to give his consent as long as he lived. But Teresa had a mind of her own, and, despite the deep affection between daughter and father, Teresa eased away from the house without his permission and entered a Carmelite convent nearby outside Avila.

During Teresa's novitiate her frail health continued to be a serious problem. She made her profession at the age of 20, and after this her sickness seemed to worsen, with frequent faintings and heart pains so severe she sometimes lost consciousness. When physicians could neither diagnose nor cure her condition, her father got her removed from the convent and placed under the care of some outstanding physicians without. But her condition worsened all the more, and for three months she was unable to rest because of a continual burning fever. As her fever continued unabated, excruciating pains developed throughout her body, and, as even her physicians seemed to give up hope, she herself entered a deep melancholic state. She began concentrating upon reading the book of Job and voicing aloud many of his words of faith in the face of suffering. In August 1537 she entered a coma that lasted four days, and because it looked as if she had died a grave was dug for her in the convent cemetery. She would have been buried if her father had not opposed it, insisting that he still could see in her certain signs of life.

Eventually Teresa regained enough consciousness to beg that her pain-wracked body, now reduced to skin and bones, be removed to the convent. At the convent she lingered between life and death for about eight months and even after that remained a cripple for more than two years. During the latter part of the time she was able to crawl about on her hands and feet, but all at once she found herself perfectly restored to health. Later it was revealed to her that God had decided that she had suffered enough for now and so had decided to relieve her from her crippled status. Meanwhile she remained well liked by her acquaintances because of her obvious love for them, and because of her strict habit held since infancy of refusing in her presence to allow even a hint of criticism of others. She insisted that others be spoken of as she wanted others to speak of her.

Though cured of her crippling disease, Teresa's health continued to be frail, and from time to time she suffered various severe maladies. Her devout father, to whom she was devoted, took sick also, and began suffering from an excruciating pain in his shoulders. Teresa advised him that since he had long been devoted to the veneration of Christ carrying the cross, he now

126

should realize that Christ, in his great mercy, was simply giving him a feeling of some part of that suffering. Teresa's reassurance comforted her father so much he never again mentioned his pain. Instead his religious devotion increased throughout the remainder of his life. In 1539 he died while saying the creed.

Teresa was both intelligent and well read and her love for people carried over to an enjoyment of talking with them and they with her. But one day as she worshipped, reciting a hymn, an unseen voice said to her, "I will not have thee hold conversations with men, but with angels." After she overcame her astonishment at this voice, she henceforth renounced all conversations with mortals except for business or the direct service of God. Hearing this voice was the first of many such occurrences, and Teresa always described the voices as being clearer and more distinct than normal. Such occurrences caused her to be greatly ridiculed by members of the convent or other members of the church, who considered her either hypocritical, deluded by the devil, or overly emotional. But she continued to labor in charity and patience and forgiveness, and one day an unseen voice again spoke to her. As she recorded in her autobiography, for the most part completed in 1562, 20 years before her death, this voice said, "Fear not, daughter, for it is I, and I will not forsake thee: do not fear." The voice reassured her, and then from time to time Christ himself appeared to her. On one occasion when she held in her hands the cross at the end of her beads, Christ took it into his hand, and then, when he returned it to her, it appeared to be of four great stones much more precious in appearance than diamonds. They had the five wounds of Christ engraved upon them in what she considered a most curious manner. After this, instead of the cross at the end of her beads she saw only the precious stones.

Teresa began maintaining an unceasing state of prayer in her life, and even while asleep she prayed to Christ. Her communion with Christ became so powerful that her soul itself began to be carried away, and she found that she was unable to stop it. As she described it, "Sometimes my whole body was carried with it, so as to be raised up from the ground, though this was seldom. When I had a mind to resist these raptures, there seemed to me somewhat of so mighty force under my feet, which raised me up, that I know not what to compare it to. All my resistance availed little; for when our Lord hath a mind to do a thing, no power is able to stand against it." Then one day as Teresa was about to receive communion from a bishop, he and others in the group observed in amazement as she rose upward out of reach of his hand. On another occasion, as she was in the choir in public view, she began to rise so high she was forced to grab hold of some rails for support, and she prayed aloud, "Lord, suffer not, for such a favour, a wicked woman to pass for virtuous." This happened at other times in the public choir until at last, because of her fervent request, this never again happened to her in public during the last 15 years of her life. While she was in these intense spiritual states she says that Christ at times revealed to her many remarkable things. She wrote that with the help of these experiences she developed such a contempt for the world and such a desire for heaven, "I lost the fear of death, of which I had formerly a great apprehension." She added that she learned great heavenly mysteries and things to come, which she foretold, and she says that of the many things revealed to her, even to the tiniest, every single thing came to pass as she predicted they would.

Sometimes she saw angels only in vague forms, but at other times in distinct bodily forms. Among the latter was a rather small but beautiful angel whose face was so inflamed and who seemed so on fire with divine love that she decided he was one of that highest order of angels known as seraphim. She wrote that "He had in his hand a long golden dart. . .and I conceived that he thrust it several times through my heart after such a manner that it passed through my very bowels; and when he drew it out, methought it pulled them out with it, and left me wholly inflamed with a great love of God." This wound caused great pain in her soul, which also affected her body; but this extremity of pain was accompanied by excessive delight. As she wrote further, "It comforts me also to hear the clock strike; for so methinks I draw a little nearer to the seeing of God; since one hour more of my life is past." She saw virtue in everyone and considered no one in the world worse than herself. Her desire for self-mortification resulted in rigorous disciplines, hair cloths, and, despite her frail health, fasts that lasted eight months out of the year. Without exception she spoke with respect and affection for those persecutors who considered her a fake, and she always gave a pious motive to their criticism, insisting that they were her best of friends and perfect servants of God. She often would describe those who reviled her as the only people who really knew her. When hearing of accusations against her she would answer with a smile, "No music is so agreeable to my ears. They have reason for what they say, and speak truth."

Teresa observed that all religious persons were not called to contemplation or self-mortification but that all could learn to lead a life of prayer. She advocated also that in worshipping Christ, one should remember to think of him sometimes as being a man as well as being the Son of God.

Gradually Teresa's powers came to be recognized as God-oriented rather than devil-or-self oriented. Faithful believers decided that she should establish a new convent at Avila in 1561, one dedicated to that extreme austerity and poverty in convent life she exemplified. During the building of the convent a wall fell and crushed a child, but when his lifeless form was brought to Teresa she took him in her arms and after some minutes of prayer restored him completely well to his mother. This convent and the miracle marked the auspicious beginning of the great church organizational work to be performed by Teresa. She lived to see the founding of 16 nunneries of her Reformed Order and 14 convents of Carmelite friars.

On September 30, 1582, one of many violent attacks of illness that occurred throughout her life forced her to her bed for the last time. On October 1 she made her confession. On the third day the holy viaticum was brought into her chamber, and despite her extreme weakness she sprang up in bed and exclaimed, "O my Lord and my spouse, the desired hour is now come. It is now time for me to depart hence. Thy will be done. The hour is at last come wherein I shall pass out of this exile, and my soul shall enjoy in thy company what it hath so earnestly longed for." Later that evening she desired and received extreme unction. After this she remained in a trancelike state for 14 hours, holding a crucifix in her hand, and died gently at nine o'clock on the evening of October 4, 1582. She had lived 67 years, six months, and seven days a life of religious devotion from her earliest years onward. It was ordered from Rome in 1586 that her remains be transferred from Avila to Alva, and when this was done it was discovered that Teresa still had her entire body with the body color natural, and the joints flexible. There at Alva her body has remained uncorrupted to this modern era. The former earthly owner of that body was canonized by the Catholic church in 1621.

For three-and-a-half centuries Teresa has been cited as one of the world's greatest examples of a person withdrawing from the normal world to a cloistered life that overcame the world. The world perhaps recognizes her name more than others supernaturally gifted in her general era, such as Colette de Corbie, Guillemette de la Rochelle, and Saint Catherine of Siena, all of whom had the levitationist's ability to overcome gravity. The Catholic church considers Teresa's story of her life to be one of history's all-time great autobiographies. Because of her many significant supernatural achievements few saints canonized by the church are better known for their supernatural records. (A detailed firsthand account of the life of Teresa is in her autobiography, over the centuries translated into many languages and published by various publishing firms. A fascinating summary account of the life of St. Teresa, as well as those of many other saints, is in the four-volume *Lives of The Saints*, Alban Butler, the Catholic Press, 1956.)

Teresa of Avila.

Serving As The Vessel For Billions Of Faithful

ABRAHAM (circa 2000-1825 B.C.). Mesopotamia (Iraq today). The community known as Ur of the Chaldeans.

Mesopotamia was on the east side of the land of Canaan, today known as the Holy Land, and on the west side was Egypt. In the year 2000 B.C. Mesopotamia and Egypt had high degrees of culture. Between them Canaan, a "land of milk and honey," was agrarian, sparsely settled, and less advanced in civilization than thriving Mesopotamia and Egypt. At an earlier age in the area of Mesopotamia at least one man had worshipped a single God. His name had been Noah, and the God he worshipped had advised him to build and stock an ark, which Noah did. Thus Noah and his entourage survived a 40-day flood and landed safely on Mount Ararat, thought to be the Mount Ararat in eastern Turkey. But after Noah's death there were no other Noahs, and the worship of many gods flourished. The Sumerian civilization was the first known civilization to flourish in the Mesopotamia area after the time of Noah. They were an extremely ancient people, and we have no knowledge of the time when they first roamed the area singly or as members of a savage tribe. We know them from the fourth millennium B.C. (4000-3000 B.C.), and already they were a civilized people owning great and large cities with skillfully constructed buildings and streets, well-prepared religious and civic organizations, and among other advancements a complicated system of writing.

About 2360-2180 B.C. the Sumerians in the Mesopotamia area had to step aside for powerful new people who gained control in the "Old Akkadian" period, named for the city of Akkad, their central city of the time. The Old Akkadian period was known for its high level of art as well as its high level of writing, borrowed among other things from the Sumerians. The popular and dominant people in the Old Akkadian period in Mesopotamia were the Semites. After a brief period the Sumerians returned to power, around 2070-1960 B.C., and for revenge and power the Sumerians this time became anti-Semitic. It was into this area and era of worshipping many gods, at a time of rising anti-Semitism, that Abraham was born into a Semitic family. His father Terah first named his son Abram. The family, probably including Abram himself at the beginning, worshipped false gods. According to Joshua 24:2 in the Old Testament of the Bible, "Your fathers lived of old beyond the Euphrates, Terah, the father of Abraham and of Nahor; and they served other gods." In fact the word Terah in the Hebrew language is related to the word "moon," and probably Abra- -ham's father was named Terah in honor of the moon god, the patron god of the city of Ur. In fact travelers to modern Ur have reported that, except for the few mud buildings, little is left but the moon at this barren place out in the middle of a desert.

Though Abram grew up amidst the worship of false gods, quite likely there were stories of creation and the flood and allegiance to one God that had been handed down by word of mouth. When they came into Ur out of the nomadic life of the desert, the Semites could well have brought stories with them that had been handed down from generation to generation as told around campfires in front of desert tents. We do know that the Sumerians and others at this time were handing down stories, however different from the Hebrew account, of creation followed by a flood from which one family survived. Certainly all along there must have been the keeping of the Biblical account, because it is preserved for us in the Bible. Therefore, even though his family had been worshipping false gods, Abram may not have been totally unprepared when events began moving him toward the worship of one God. Perhaps because of anti-Semitism from the Sumerians, the father Terah took his son Abram and three other family members to the city of Haran, part way to Canaan. Terah died in Haran, and after the death of Abram's father God told Abram, as related at the beginning of the twelfth chapter of Genesis: "Leave your own country behind you, and your own people, and go to the land I will guide you to. If you do, I will cause you to become the father of a great nation; I will bless you and make your name famous, and you will be a blessing to many others. I will bless those who bless you and curse those who curse you; and the entire world will be blessed because of you."

Abram obeyed God's request to enter Canaan, and after witnessing with increased faith God's destruction, creation, and restoration of life, he received permanent tenure in Canaan's Promised Land. Unwitting centerpiece in the first such destruction was Pharaoh of Egypt. Abram had by now married Abram's own "very beautiful" though half-sister Sarai. Because Canaan endured a terrible famine, Abram fled with his household to an Egypt that already had reached one of its peaks in history. Four thousand years before Christ and hence two thousand years before Abram, the Egyptians were refining copper and making pottery, were living in villages, and were plying the Nile in boats. The greatest of the Great Pyramids already was 700 years old by Abram's time. But despite all the Egyptian antiquity the Pharoah remained young at heart, and, hearing the palace guards praise the beauty of Sarai, he had her brought to his harem. Even though the Pharoah gave Abram many gifts because of her—sheep, oxen, donkeys, men and women slaves, and camels—neither God nor Abram were placated. God sent a terrible plague on Pharoah's household (Genesis 12:17), as a result of which Pharoah promptly got the message and sent Abram and his household and all their possessions out of Egypt under armed escort.

Even more severe was the next destruction observed by Abram after moving to Canaan. Abram's nephew Lot and his family had settled to the east of Abram in the fertile Jordan River valley near the city of Sodom. Sodom was an extremely wicked city, the men among other things raping other men who ventured into their city. God decided to destroy Sodom and told Lot and his household to leave the area and not look back. Lot and his household fled, but as God rained down fire from heaven upon Sodom and a nearby other wicked city named Gomorrah, along with other cities and villages of the plain, Lot's wife looked back and was turned into a pillar of salt. Meanwhile Abram looked eastward out of Canaan across the plains to Sodom and Gomorrah and saw the columns of smoke and fumes, as from a furnace, rising from the cities there.

Even as Abram witnessed God's power against the wrongs in Egypt, Sodom, and Gomorrah, God kept promising great things for him. When Abram was 99 years old, God appeared to him and told him, ". . . you shall be the father of not only one nation, but a multitude of nations." Abram fell face downward in the dust as God talked with him. "What's more," God told him, "I am changing your name. It is no longer 'Abram' ('Exalted Father'), but 'Abraham' ('Father of Nations')—for that is what you will be" (Genesis 17:5). "And I will give all this land of Canaan to you and them, forever." God added that, "Your part of the contract is that you personally and all your posterity have this continual responsibility: that every male among you shall be circumcised; the foreskin of his penis shall be cut off. This will be the proof that you and they accept this covenant. Every male shall be circumsized on the eighth day after birth . . . . all must be circumsized. Your bodies will thus be marked as participants in my everlasting covenant." Then God added, "Regarding Sarai your wife—her name is no longer 'Sarai' but 'Sarah' ('Princess'). And I will bless her and give you a son from her!" But at this Abraham threw himself down in disbelief! "Me, be a father?' he said in amusement. "Me—100 years old? And Sarah, to have a baby at 90?" God reassured him that at about this same time next year he indeed would have a son and that his name would be Isaac ('Laughter'). That very day Abraham took every male and cut off their foreskins as Abraham's part of the covenant (Genesis 17:23). And Sarah did in fact become pregnant and the following year, when Abraham was 100, gave him a son whom they named Isaac (Genesis 21:1).

After Abraham had witnessed God's destruction of life and then creation of it, Abraham's faith seemed ready for its ultimate test. Through Isaac his father's seed indeed could be passed along to others. Yet when God one day demanded of Abraham that he sacrifice this very son Isaac, "The next morning Abraham got up early, chopped wood for a fire upon the altar, saddled his donkey, and took with him his son Isaac and

The greatest of the pyramids in nearby Egypt already was 700 years old by the time of Abraham.

two young men who were his servants, and started off to the place where God had told him to go" (Genesis 22:1-4). Then on the third day when Abraham saw the place in the distance, he and Isaac went forward together. "Father," Isaac asked, "we have the wood and the flint to make the fire, but where is the lamb for the sacrifice?" "God will see to it, my son," Abraham replied. And they went on. When they arrived at the place where God had told Abraham to go, he built an altar and placed the wood in order, ready for the fire, and then tied Isaac and laid him on the altar over the wood. And Abraham took the knife and lifted it up to plunge it into his son, to slay him. At that moment the Angel of God shouted to him from Heaven, "Lay down the knife; don't hurt the lad in any way, for I know God is first in your life—you have not withheld even your beloved son from me."

Thus Abraham offered his human son as a sacrifice even as God later would offer His son Christ. Undoubtedly Abraham had the faith that even if he had killed Isaac, God would have raised him from the dead, as God indeed did later with Christ. Thus out of great faith Abraham became a father of multitudes, and in fact three of today's largest religious groups claim him as founder: Judaism, Islam, and Christianity. (A widely accepted Bible made easy to read for modern readers is *The Living Bible: Paraphrased*, Tyndale House Publishers, 1971. An account of many interesting characters in the Bible can be found in *Great Personalities Of The Bible*, William Sanford LaSor, Fleming H. Revell, 1965.)

Starting A Spiritual Revolution Sans Clothing

MAHAVIRA (circa 600 B.C.). India. Bihar.

His parents were such devout ascetics they finally fasted to death. At age 30 Mahavira, or "Great Man," renounced a life of ease and plenty, pulled out all his hair, and began to roam clad in a single robe. Later he discarded this minor clothing and traveled about nude. In a devout struggle to avoid injury or other evil to anything, he swept clean the paths before him to avoid stepping on insects, wore a cloth over his mouth in order to avoid drawing insects into his mouth when he breathed, and strained his food with a cloth. He slept little as he roamed the Indian countryside for 12 years, seeking to liberate himself from the false worship of life. At last he stopped at a river bank where he began sitting under a tree near an old temple. He meditated there until he obtained complete isolation of his soul, the knowledge of complete spirituality. In this manner he became a Jina, a conqueror of evil.

Now that he had obtained a sublime state for himself he began preaching his gospel to others, doing so for the next 30 years. He had great success among the Jina believers, epitomizing for them their belief that a true Jina is a conqueror of evil. The Jinas grew to consider Mahavira the last in a long line of 24 Jinas in the present world era. The first Jina, named Rishaba, had lived millions of years ago. And now around the sixth century B.C. had come Mahavira, the last. So great was Mahavira's success throughout India he attracted 50,000 monks and 500,000 lay devotees.

Today the Jina religion, even though a relatively small religious minority, has about a million and a half adherents, all rejecting the Hindu Vedas and most Hindu gods and instead substituting their own scriptures for those of Hinduism. Their main similarity with either Hinduism or Buddhism is that the Jina religionists too believe in karma (deeds) and rebirth. But they alone are known for their strong belief in life-nomads, or multitudes of souls that are all independent and eternal. And the last manifestation, Mahavira, among 24 Jinas who completely conquered soul and overcame evil, led a life of self denial that included worshipping in the nude to show disrespect for his body. Mahavira is the last Jinas example for the Jina worshippers, whose principal practice is meditation as they contemplate the good nature of the Jinas and try to follow their example by vowing to avoid injury and evil.

This huge statue in Mysore, India, is a representative of the strength over evil epitomized by Mahavira and his followers.

139

Taking Temporary Grasp Of Timeless Power

AIMEE SEMPLE McPHERSON (A.D. October 9, 1890-September 27, 1944). Canada. Ontario. A farm near Ingersill.

Aimee's mother, Mrs. Minnie Kennedy, before becoming a farm wife and mother had worked religiously as a Salvation Army lass. Even before Aimee was born Minnie Kennedy prayed earnestly that her forthcoming child would become a woman preacher, and when baby Aimee was only a few weeks old her mother trundled her to the nearest Salvation Army barracks and dedicated young Aimee to the service of the Lord. Aimee's farmer father, like her mother, was a devout follower of the spirited Pentecostal Holiness religion. Aimee grew up to be an attractive looking, high-spirited young girl who especially enjoyed swimming and riding horseback on the farm.

Although prayer, Bible reading, church attendance, and moral living was a hallmark of her home life, it was a so-called "neighborhood Holy Roller Pentecostal Revival" that fully clarified for Aimee her life's mission. As the handsome young revivalist named Robert Semple shouted "Repent" to the farm families gathered in the stark meeting hall, Aimee was among those listening well. But the girl remained unaware of the full impact of the revival upon her until one night at home she leaned from her bedroom window and had an experience that she would relate to millions in years forthcoming. "It was like a shaft of light shooting through the darkness—like the rending of the temple from the top to the bottom—like the brushing of all the cobwebs from the mind, as though from the cellar I had been lifted to the housetop under the shining of the open heavens." An overriding sense of guilt seemed to permeate her very being for three full days. Then at the end of three days when she felt like she could stand it no longer, a second spectacular experience occurred that seemed to free her fully from her sense of guilt. As she drove home from school, "It seemed that the heavens were brass and would fall upon me and I would be lost if I did not immediately repent of my unbelief and Christ's rejection." Lifting her hands toward heaven she cried aloud, "God, be merciful to me, a sinner." With this, "The light streamed over my soul . . . .My fear was gone and in its place there was a blessed rest. . . .I consecrated my life to Christ then and there. I have never done anything halfheartedly . . . ."

Arriving home after her eventful car ride from school, Aimee Kennedy swept all the secular music off her piano. And as she had replaced secular music with hymnals, she replaced her secular reading with reading of her Bible. She took her Bible to school with her, even concealing it inside her algebra book, and in addition to her regular worship she attended prayer meetings in a nearby cottage. Young Semple returned and visited the Kennedy farm where Aimee joyfully shared with him the full account of her conversion. The young evangelist was caught up in the animation of the girl's account and, at the same time, found himself enamored with the girl herself. Soon he asked her to marry him and as his wife to accompany him as missionaries to China. "I said 'Yes' to God and I said 'Yes' to Robert," Aimee later recalled. They were married at the farm home, and their wedding feast was held among the apple trees in the orchard.

In the short time between their marriage and their departure for China the young Semples were an active husband-and-wife ministerial team, the husband preaching and Aimee playing the piano, leading the hymns, and testifying. But their happiness together was short-lived. The couple barely had arrived in China, starting together on their missionary campaign, when Semple developed fever and ague. They were in Hong Kong when he died, a month before a daughter was born. Soon after Aimee returned to Ontario to live with her daughter, Aimee's father died of a stroke. Her mother rejoined her first love, the Salvation Army, this time serving with the Army in the United

141

Aimee Semple McPherson.

States in New York. Aimee, remaining in Ontario, married her second husband, a grocery clerk named Harold S. McPherson. She persuaded him to leave the position of grocery clerk and become a traveling evangelist with her. They moved around Ontario, preaching to farmers, but McPherson could not adjust to this drastic change in life style nor understand why his wife would not settle down as a housewife like other women. When they separated in 1916 he sent her the message, "I have tried to walk your way and have failed. Won't you come now and walk my way? I am sure we would be happy." But Aimee found she could make no choice other than follow the life to which she had been dedicated even before birth.

Within six years after the separation between her and her husband in 1916, the vivacious young evangelist earned a worldwide reputation as a leading exponent of that fundamental type of religion that she called Four Square Gospel. Conducting increasingly popular tent revivals, gaining more and more reputation for divine healing, she traveled south from Ontario into the United States through the state of Maine and on south to Florida. Her methods at first suggested her rustic background and perhaps a carry-over of Salvation Army influence from her mother. She painted makeshift signs which she displayed from her old car. In fact at Key West in Florida, Mrs. Kennedy did join her daughter and bring firsthand her experience of doing much with little in an organized religious movement. Before long mother and daughter were touring in a well-organized caravan with agents in advance paving the way.

Yet despite the increasing organization, it continued to be an individualistic Aimee crusade. Rather than the fundamental emotionalism of her mother's fire-and-brimstone Holiness allegiance, Aimee moved more and more toward espousing a religion of positive thinking, her joyful approach to Christianity doubly enhanced by her naturally buoyant charismatic personality. She did it her way. As one example, she would stand motionless at a street corner, her arms lifted in reverance, her eyes closed in prayer. As soon as a crowd collected she would come to life with the words, "Follow me," and hurry toward her meeting place, be it tent, hall, or church. And they began following. Sometimes she would use a megaphone to startle passersby with the loud exhortation, "Do you know that you are on your way to perdition?" In St. Petersburg, Florida, during Mardi Gras she exuberantly created her own float and joined the parade. From her car she displayed white sheets with signs printed on the sheets reading: "Jesus Saves!" "Repent And Be Converted!" "I'm On The Way To The Tent Revival. R.U.?" The crowd stared, but before long many of the revellers were following her to the meeting.

It was not until after the Aimee Semple McPherson Crusade reached Los Angeles, California, in 1918, however, that it climbed to the heights from which its fame spread worldwide.

The traveling revival group first met in a hall, then in a church, and finally in the Philharmonic Auditorium in order to accommodate the thousands flocking in to hear the exciting woman evangelist with the reputation growing worldwide. Successful in Los Angeles, she used it as her headquarters from which to make national and international tours, including four transcontinental tours and crusades in Canada, New Zealand, and Australia. Her revival sites spanned the spectrum from churches to schools to a huge tent, and even the San Francisco Coliseum proved barely large enough to accommodate the crowds that flocked to hear her messages. Faith healing became more and more a part of her ministry. In the summer of 1921, the same year, incidently, that her husband finally divorced her for desertion, 8,000 crowded into her opening meeting at San Jose, California. It was a mass display of healing that was reported around the world. Among the many healed were crippled or blinded veterans from World War I who made newspaper headlines as they reported restoration of vision or limb. Crutches, canes, and braces were stacked high on the platform around Aimee. This was repeated on many occasions in many places.

Yet as the healing fame of Mrs. McPherson spread, so did the criticism. She was ordained a pastor in the First Baptist Church of San Jose. Even though there was a resurging movement of laying on of hands and other divine healing methods, from as different religions as the so-called non-emotional Episcopalians and the emotional Pentecostal Holiness, most of the in-between denominations including the Baptist showed a surprising divine-healing suspicion. Faced on one hand with growing ridicule not only from outside but from within her own denomination, and on the other faced with an amazing spread of fame that apparently did not depend upon divine healing, Aimee did a startling thing. She announced to reporters in San Francisco in the spring of 1922 that "I say very definitely, right now, that I do not wish the lame, the halt, the blind and the crippled to crowd my meetings. I hope they will stay away . . . . That is the portion of my work to which I am least attracted . . . ."

The next four climactic years, after announcing that she did not want the afflicted to crowd her meetings, the fame of Aimee Semple McPherson continued to spread. She announced plans to build the huge Angelus Temple in Los Angeles, funds poured in, and in this massive white building with its five entrances and seating capacity for more than 5,000, Aimee Semple McPherson began preaching to a congregation said to be the world's largest. By the end of 1925, with Aimee at age 35, her collections there were reported to have reached a million dollars, the value of the church property itself a reported half million. Never did the Temple lights go out nor its doors close. In two-hour shifts in the Watch Tower women prayed all day, and men prayed all night. The church had 24 departments and a Bible School with a thousand students. Included among its many musical groups were three bands, three choirs, and two orchestras. Special electric trains ran to the Temple. Nor did Aimee forget her traveling evangelism. One such tour was to Denver, Colorado, where 2,800 people arose and moved forward in a solid body.

Aimee Semple McPherson's pinnacle of success extended four years after her San Francisco announcement regarding the lame, the halt, the blind, and the crippled. Then on May 19, 1926, the world was shocked to hear that Aimee had drowned while swimming at a beach near Los Angeles. It was even more shocked when she returned the following month on June 23 and explained that she'd been kidnapped. But though the throng of faithful yelling "Aimee! Aimee! Hallelujah!" greeted her return to Angelus Temple, millions of nonfaithful including investigative authorities and worldwide communicators began chopping away at her kidnapping report. Asking more and more embarrassing questions, they accused her of a month's sexual interlude in hiding with one of her employees, a married radio engineer. Week after week one crisis of accusation followed another; just as one court battle disappeared another began to surface. Friend in the Angelus Temple turned against friend. Some reported that Aimee's own mother, who had dedicated her now famous daughter to the ministry even before birth, had become Aimee's worst enemy. It was reported widely that Aimee refused to have her picture taken with her mother. And that her mother, with a battered nose in a hospital, had charged daughter Aimee with knocking her down and threatening to have her killed. Many claimed that for good measure her mother announced that while on a European tour her daughter had gone to a doctor and had her face lifted. Though Aimee vehemently denied it in front page stories, the name of the plastic surgeon, the price he had charged, and all the incriminating details soon were widely reported.

And though Aimee fought valiantly to rededicate her life to preaching the Gospel as effectively as before the disappearance, it never worked that way. On September 12, 1931, she married her third husband, David L. Hutton, a baritone at the Temple. But Hutton divorced her two years later, reportedly claiming that she had pulled a hoax on him by pretending that she was going to have a baby. Meanwhile her mother, former Salvation Army lass Mrs. Kennedy, eloped with a man whom she later divorced. All in all, it was not the kind of publicity a minister looks for. As Aimee and many faithful continued to insist that she was falsely accused, and that things at the Temple were better than publicized, accusations increased. Once Aimee asked a reporter why a paper printed most of the negative and rarely anything of the positive, and he answered, "Aimee good! That's no news. Aimee bad! Wow."

Aimee Semple McPherson continued to preach at the Temple and elsewhere, and in 1944, at age 54, died in a hotel in Oakland, California, where she had delivered a lecture the night before. Her death was diagnosed as an accidental overdose of sleeping pills. Thousands flocked past her bier in Angelus Temple, including 1,500 ministers who had been ordained by her. A marble vault, fronted by two life-sized angels, guarded her coffin. The Temple, under the pastorship of her son Rolf, continued to flourish. and her October 9 birthday continued to be celebrated at the Temple. Though in later years her life had been beset by human problems, for a while that same body had proved to be a vessel for unlimited power. (For an interesting comparison of Aimee Semple McPherson and other famous Americans read *Charmers & Cranks Twelve Famous American Women Who Defied The Conventions*, Ishbel Ross, Harper & Row, 1965. A study more acceptable to the Aimee Semple McPherson faithful is in a manuscript underway entitled *Guilty Until Proved Innocent* by Dr. Raymond L. Cox, pastor of the Salem, Oregon, Foursquare Church.)

Talking With Another Adult Nine Times Larger

> **ZOROASTER (630-553 B.C.) Persia. Medina.**

Born to the warrior clan of Spitama he was given the name Zarathushtra. The Greeks changed his name to Zoroaster, a name easier to pronounce. Zoroaster was born during the world-wide era of great spiritual awakening in the sixth and fifth centuries B.C. Miraculous events were associated with his birth. A light shone throughout the heavens, illuminating the laughing newborn, and evil spirits fled in terror. Despite his militaristic background Zoroaster throughout his life seemed driven by a spiritual desire to seek goodness and understanding.

At about age 40 he found himself in the presence of a figure approximately nine times human size. This figure was Vohu Mana (Good Mind) who directed him into the presence of Ahura Mazda (Wise Lord). It was a call for Zoroaster to become a divine teacher. Although Zoroaster left this meeting not entirely convinced, eventually he gave himself completely to the task. At one point he rid himself of an enemy spirit by hurling sacred texts at him. For ten years Zoroaster denounced idolatry and evil living and proclaimed faith in one god, Ahura Mazda. But for these ten years he made no converts except one, his cousin. Finally he journeyed east to Bactri where he converted the king of that land. After years of preaching, Zoroaster was killed by some priests near a fire-altar.

A thousand years after the death of the prophet the Zoroastrian religion was so widely accepted it became the official religion of the Persian state. The Greeks and Romans called it the religion of the Magi (the wise men of the Bible nativity story). Some of the Magi emigrated to India and East Africa where the religion continues to thrive and prosper. Followers of Zoroaster's religion are known today primarily by the name Parsis or Gabars. It continues to be the only one of the world's great religions that closes its places of worship to outsiders, including visitors. Outsiders call the Parsi places of worship "fire temples." Today only a hundred thousand or so people follow this historic religion, founded by a leader who began his spiritual mission after talking with another nine times human size.

Testing Beyond Genius Level

GERARD CROISET (A.D. March 10, 1909-   ).
Holland. Laren.

Gerard was born to Jewish parents who traveled with a theatre group. As a prominent actor, his father Hyman toured Holland and Belgium playing leading roles in Shakespeare and Ibsen dramas. Gerard's mother was a mistress of wardrobes. The attractive Hyman was considered "a ladies' man," who from time to time deserted and then returned to live with Gerard's mother, with whom he had a common-law marriage. Gerard's father espoused atheism and socialism and otherwise became known as an individualist among fellow Hollanders.

Gerard's home had almost no home life. He grew to hate as well as love his father, especially after his parents put him in a foster home at age eight, where his unhappy childhood worsened. During childhood he lived with six different sets of foster parents, all of whom he irritated. They in turn punished the youngster excessively. On more than one occasion one foster father would force the rebellious youth to a stake in the floor and chain him by the leg. Disease increased the child's unhappiness as rickets wracked his frail body.

To escape his misery Gerard began losing himself in daydreaming. Adults considered him increasingly strange as he began reporting strange playmates visible only to himself. Also, from time to time he would startle others by vocalizing their private thoughts. By school age Gerard was convinced that he was different. Moving from one foster home to another, he re-

149

ceived little formal education. One of his infrequent teachers even questioned his ability to learn, only to have Gerard amaze him by describing the teacher's actions while absent from the classroom.

At age eight Gerard slipped and fell into one of Holland's many waterways and almost drowned. Only at the last minute was he rescued. When the man who rescued him fell from a ladder and died within the next few months, Gerard went into deep despair. He felt guilty for not being there to catch him when he fell, thereby saving the man as the man had saved him.

After the various foster homes, Gerard entered an orphanage. But because he rebelled against orphanage rules he fought a running battle with the superintendent, who at times would give him severe beatings with a cane or would lock him in a small room. The punishments led to even deeper resentment and hostility on the boy's part. A different kind of trauma came one day after a child dropped several coins. Gerard, pretending to help look, hid one of the coins under a foot. When the distraught child left after an unsuccessful search, Gerard moved his foot, picked up the coin, and kept it for two days. Conscience-stricken almost from the moment he hid the coin, he returned it to the rightful owner with the excuse that he had found it where the other had lost it.

When a girl classmate fell in the schoolyard and hurt herself, 11-year-old Gerard reacted without thinking by placing a consoling hand upon her injured leg. The teacher, misunderstanding Gerard's act, thought he meant to touch the girl lewdly and whipped the youth. The following year he felt an urge to help his arthritic grandmother, for whom he had close affection, by stroking her limbs where the arthritis hurt.

By the time Gerard was 11, his actor father had deserted his mother once and for all and she legally married another man. Gerard returned to live with them, but continuous friction resulted between him and his stepfather, and Gerard ran away from home often. At age 13 he left school again, this time to work for a farmer in return for room and board and clothes. But farm life bored him, and he quit this time to work as a junior clerk in the office of a harbor master. Before he had a chance to quit this job because of boredom, the harbor master instigated the termination, firing him because of his inaccuracy

Gerard Croiset, shown here, has friends among policemen in many countries.

World pioneer in the scientific testing of the Gerard Croisets of this world, who are gifted beyond the natural, is Dr. W. H. C. Tenhaeff, shown here, of the State University of Utrecht in Holland.

in adding figures. Thus in youth he went from one job to another. Successful in none, he had been a shop assistant, a salesman, a clerk, a farmhand, and a grocery store helper.

In 1934, now at age 25, Croiset married a carpenter's daughter whom he had dated for four years. Croiset had difficulty supporting his wife and their son Hyman born a year after their marriage. So his wife's family helped him open a grocery store; but his lack of business ability plus his generous habit of extending credit, or giving rather than selling, led to the store's bankruptcy. The failure of his grocery store in 1935 depressed Croiset so much he had a nervous breakdown.

In the face of deep despair, Croiset began to concentrate on his supernatural abilities. One day the forlorn storekeeper, now bankrupt, was seated beside a road when a former customer halted his bicycle to ask Croiset if he needed help. After listening to Croiset's troubles the former customer invited him to visit him and his wife that evening. Croiset jumped at the opportunity for a sympathetic audience, and in their home that evening Croiset told them about some of his past supernatural experiences. His host, a spiritualist, accepted the accounts and invited Croiset to attend spiritualist sessions where seances were conducted. Croiset did for a while before his independent nature directed him away from such group gatherings.

Croiset's public mission in the history of the supernatural began in 1935 when he and his wife visited a watchmaker. On a whim Croiset lifted a meter stick off a table, and at once images of the watchmaker's youth flashed into Croiset's mind. Croiset began a detailed recounting of significant events in the watchmaker's youth, including even a detailed description of where a participant's body landed following an early automobile accident that had been traumatic for the watchmaker. The watchmaker exclaimed that Croiset was a clairvoyant and afterwards apparently talked as much as barbers in other climes. At least people started bringing Croiset their problems, and, forgetting about his bankruptcy, he began concentrating on helping them.

On various occasions and to the disbelief of most or all who heard, Croiset predicted a future Nazi invasion of Holland. After the Nazis did, indeed, occupy Holland in May 1940, they compelled him with other Jews to wear a Jewish-star armband. Though he had the opportunity to conceal his Jewish origin through false papers, he refused. And when the Nazis refused to let Jews have bicycles, he bought a pair of roller skates and traversed the town by skating. In 1941, at age 32, there came to his mind an image of his impending arrest by the Nazis. He sought neighborhood help in hiding his wife and children, but in his own case an inner voice told him to continue his work in Holland instead of going into hiding. Two weeks later about five o'clock on a Sunday morning the Gestapo came to his home and arrested him. Rounding him up with many other Jews, plus a few non-Jewish Dutchmen, they shipped them to Germany. During the trip Croiset found himself so enraged by the brutality of the Nazi guards, fellow prisoners had to restrain him forcibly from fighting back, and because of them his life probably was spared.

For no apparent reason the Nazis freed Croiset in 1943, and he returned to his home in Holland. Though his papers already showed that he was married to a non-Jew, his friends, now hoping to save him from a second arrest, falsified his documents to show that his mother was non-Jewish. The safety of Croiset was in the public interest. He was using his clairvoyant ability to help others escape the Nazis. An example was his passing a house one day and sensing that Jews were hiding inside and that Nazis would soon raid them. At his warning the Dutch underground became involved, and when the Nazis raided the house the Jews already had fled to safety.

In late 1943 the Nazis again arrested Croiset, as part of a non-Jewish as well as Jewish Dutch labor force for deportation to Germany. Though the journey became a nightmare, with long forced marches and much starvation, Croiset again survived. And several months later, again without explanation, the Nazis allowed him to return to his home in Holland.

Meanwhile, among the Dutchmen caught in the Nazi dragnet was famed psychology author and instructor at the University of Utrecht, Dr. Willem Tenhaeff. Born in 1894 he had dedicated his life to studying the supernatural, and even as a young Dutch officer in the World War I era had used his off-duty hours in supernatural study. As part of his study of the abilities and techniques of fortunetellers, he visited one in 1915 who predicted with accuracy, "When you get out of the army . . . you will study and then teach. I see many students around you. But your students are grown-up people. Not children. Later I see you writing many books." By the start of World War II, the University of Utrecht luminary was well on his way toward earning his worldwide reputation, the first man in the Netherlands, and perhaps the world, to undertake the long-range, scientific qualitative research of clairvoyants.

Beginning in 1936, four years before the German invasion of Holland, Dr. Tenhaeff was including anti-Nazi material among his prolific writings. It has been estimated that Dutch students and faculty members comprised a third of the Dutch people whom the Nazis executed, and Dr. Tenhaeff escaped that fateful third with luck. Though the Nazis issued an order for his arrest, a Dutch police friend noted Dr. Tenhaeff's name on the arrest list and gave warning just in time for the doctor to go into hiding. But Dr. Tenhaeff, working with other underground instructors and students, continued his chosen work, even lecturing on the supernatural to audiences in various private homes. At the war's end Dr. Tenhaeff returned to the University of Utrecht and one evening gave a visiting lecture at Enschede. Among those attending was the unknown 36-year-old bankrupt former grocer Gerard Croiset, who afterwards requested that the doctor test his strange abilities. Thus began an association that would last decades, with Dr. Tenhaeff bringing Croiset to the University of Utrecht. For many years he had been bringing other supernaturally gifted people to the university and testing them with comprehensive programs to learn how they differed from the ordinary.

Dr. Tenhaeff learned that Croiset not only differed from the ordinary, he even differed in some marked ways from others supernaturally gifted. The doctor's many quantitative and qualitative profiles over the years had come to show that the average gifted (permitted the word average) was childlike, talkative, tense, and, even more surprising, suffered from a stomach disorder. Though all this applied to Croiset, who wears loose clothing because of stomach pains that include a chronic ulcer, he also shows unusual aggressiveness and vanity, perhaps because of his childhood. Above all, Croiset's supernatural powers were the most consistent and pronounced of those of anyone tested in the long history of testing at Utrecht.

Starting near the middle of the twentieth century, Croiset's powers became so widely known, police agencies, other organizations, and ordinary citizens throughout the world began calling on Croiset to help them solve crimes or locate missing persons or other missing objects. For example, six years after the 1953 gangland slaying of a Minnesota, United States, mobster, a Minneapolis radio and television network decided to seek Croiset's help in locating the still-missing body. They sent him the mobster's photograph and a map of several counties in the St. Paul area. Croiset concentrated upon these two items and from a distance of 5,000 miles described with accuracy the details of the case. An example of another "missing case" viewed at long geographical distance involved a 60-year-old business-man who disappeared in Spain. His wife came from Madrid to Utrecht bearing the businessman's photograph and toothbrush. Croiset touched the two objects lightly, then exclaimed, "I don't want to have anything to do with this man! I don't like him a bit . . . . He really isn't worth it . . . . He isn't dead but very much alive, and he will come back." Croiset went on to describe the appearance of an alcoholic treatment hospital in Majorca, off the coast of Spain, where the businessman was hos-pitalized for delirium tremens.

Three years before Croiset helped locate the missing alco-holic in Spain, the distraught father of a missing 18-year-old girl phoned Croiset for help. Croiset reassured the father that the girl was safe in another country, Austria, and that the father would learn so in three days. Three days later the police phoned the father that his daughter indeed was safe in Austria. Croiset prophesied with similar success the following year when a news reporter phoned from Belgium for assistance in locating a miss-ing 18-year-old youth. Croiset assured the caller that the boy was safe in France, and that definite news would come within three days. The following afternoon the Belgian Consul in southern France phoned the missing boy's family that he was safe but needed money to return home to Antwerp.

Though Croiset often has been successful in helping solve thefts, he does not in general give top priority to this kind of work, and most of his solving of thefts has been in Holland rath-er than international. It is in the Netherlands that he has done the majority of his apprehension of dishonest employees, smug-glers, and even crooked cops.

For more than a quarter century Croiset has given years of unstinting work as a "supernatural guinea pig" for the Universi-ty of Utrecht and the world. He also feels a compulsion either to help find missing people or help heal the afflicted. He accepts no money for his clairvoyant work and earns his living as a healer.

Healing in general, and what is known as "laying on of hands" in some religions, comes naturally to Gerard, as had been indicated earlier with the 11-year-old girl and with his arthritic grandmother. He had even continued his healing work during World War II when a Nazi policeman dragged a reluctant

Croiset from his Enschede home across the German border to treat a Gestapo officer suffering a painful sciatic attack. Suddenly Croiset saw a glaring light which revealed the letter L and the figures 6x35. Croiset, very religious despite his nonreligious parents, recalled the Biblical words from the Gospel of St. Luke 6:35, "But love ye your enemies and do good . . ." No longer reluctant, Croiset forgot that the Nazi was an enemy and "saw only a sick man." Also in World War II, during his nearly six months in a German work camp, which had neither nurses nor doctors, Croiset treated Dutch prisoners and Nazi patients alike. A prominent feature in Croiset's home after the war became a framed testimonial signed by some of those grateful patients.

What is called supernatural healing, divine healing, faith healing, witchcraft, or magic in some nations in Holland often is known as magnetic healing. It is said that nearby France even has more such healers than medical doctors. Surveys have shown that 25 percent of Utrecht's citizens have visited magnetic healers, and Utrecht's busiest such healer is Croiset, seeing from 100 to 120 patients a day in addition to his frequent daily phone conversations with those seeking other clairvoyant help. These patients for magnetic healing who crowd Croiset's home contribute an average $1.40 for the first visit and $.70 thereafter, and their afflictions range from headache to cancer. To pinpoint the affliction he places strong, vibrating fingers over the patient's body. Though his percentage of healing is no more fail-proof than is human clairvoyancy, the success at least sometimes seeming attuned to the recipient's receptivity, his healings include various polio and paralyzed patients considered incurable by medical doctors. Often his treatment requires no more than a minute, and his patients are divided about evenly between men and women and range from the successful well knowns to poor unknowns. These latter Croiset treats with love and without charge.

As a matter of interest Croiset fulfills that oft-quoted axiom that it is much easier for a healer to heal others than himself. While healing hundreds of others, Croiset continues to suffer with stomach pains as well as pains in his legs because of severe varicose veins. He treats his own discomfort by wearing rubber stockings and daily heavy bandaging of his legs.

Though the University of Utrecht maintains a respectable

distance between its testing for clairvoyance and the more suspect magnetic healing, Holland is in a part of the world where both areas have more than normal credibility. Thus many of the thousands of case histories at the university include magnetic healing data.

In 1953 the State University of Utrecht established its Parapsychology Institute (from the Greek word "para" meaning "beyond"), and after 39 years of uphill work Dr. Willem H. C. Tenhaeff received a professorship, the world's first chair in parapsychology. That same year the University of Utrecht hosted the world's First International Conference of Parapsychological Studies, a conference sponsored by the Netherlands Minister of Education and the Parapsychology Foundation of New York, attended by ESP (extrasensory perception) delegates from 14 nations. Nucleus of all this at the University of Utrecht was the continuing hard work of the small staff of four, reaching an annual budget of $14,000, the world-renowned Professor Tenhaeff's own annual salary being only $4,200. On this basis and with the help of Croiset and many of Utrecht's other paragnosts (a word derived by Dr. Tenhaeff in part from the Greek word "gnosis" meaning "knowledge"), the university's studies not only have survived but flourished.

Croiset consistently has refused even travel compensation for his clairvoyant "gift from God." The contributions of many have led to the many thousands of tests at Utrecht, leading to startling tested conclusions. It is difficult for a skilled clairvoyant to separate the past and present and future. As most of us do in dreaming, the skilled clairvoyant tends to think in terms of pictures rather than words, to see a tree rather than to see the word tree. Tests show many children gifted with telepathy in a typical school; that girls are better at telepathy than are boys; that children from an "affectionate family background" generally guess better than those from a background of strife; that telepathy works better in a friendly classroom than a bickering one; and that so-called "high income" children from professional families of businessmen, lawyers, and doctors and the like have the least telepathic capabilities. Probable cause is that these parents are more interested in their work than in their families. By far the best telepathic results come from skilled labor or otherwise lower-income-level families.

Somehow it seems noteworthy that the greatest concentrated durable stride in the study of the supernatural received its greatest outside assist from a low-income youth bearing the scars of a tragic background. Though the supernatural is a more and more consuming study throughout the world, from nationally religious India to nonreligious though supernaturally conscious Russia, none yet but Holland has had its famous Croiset, documented with firsthand intensity for more than a quarter century. (For a detailed firsthand account by a veteran successful author who pioneered in bringing the Croiset story to the English-speaking world, read *Croiset The Clairvoyant*, Jack Harrison Pollack, Doubleday & Company, 1964.)

Transferring An Affliction
From Another To Yourself

**SRI SAI BABA OF SHIRDI (A.D. 1838-1918). India.
Shirdi.**

Sai Baba appeared at about age 16 wearing the clothes of a
Muslim holy man, in India called a fakir. When asked, the youth
revealed neither his caste nor his parentage but instead spoke
mainly in parables. He appeared unmindful of either cold or
heat. For a while the youth lived outside under the branches of
a tree. Several years passed, and then he began performing miracles such as scooping up ordinary dirt in the form of fire or water as he requested. As the fame of the young fakir spread, people began addressing him as Sai Baba, and he moved into an
abandoned Muslim mosque.

One of Sai Baba's miracles was to keep a lamp with a dry
wick burning continuously. But perhaps his best-known miracles involved healing. He cured leprosy, restored sight to the
blind, and enabled the lame to walk. One of the most unusual
aspects of his healing was his willingness to take on another's
affliction in healing. On one occasion he stuck his arm into a
fire and severely burned it before his attendants could pull him
free. He did this becuse his mind brought him the image of a
child in a distant village falling into a fire, and so immediately
he thrust his own arm into a fire, thus transferring the burn
from the child to himself. On another occasion he took another's bubonic plague and by so doing saved the afflicted layman.

In contrast to assuming the affliction of another, Sai Baba
sometimes would fly into a rage because of a devotee's action.

160

On one occasion he grabbed one of his devotees by the throat, and on another threw pieces of brick at some of them. Although such conduct might well amaze the uninitiated, it was not unusual for such spiritual guides to use unexpected methods in instructing disciples. Sai Baba became the spiritual adviser or guru for a large number of disciples.

In Hinduism complete submission to a guru's instruction is considered essential in order to obtain the knowledge of God. Sai Baba considered himself a divinity who took human form in order to instruct mankind, including the guidance of his disciples into wisdom to free them from the cycle of rebirths that had bound them. Among Sai Baba's devotees during his 60 years of spiritually instructing and physically helping others were people from all walks of life including many professionals such as government officials, court judges, lawyers, and doctors. More and more came to touch his feet and to be blessed by him.

After several occasions of indicating to his devotees his impending death, including its actual date, Sai Baba "dropped his body" on October 14, 1918. Hindu devotees believed that Sai Baba's body should be cremated in accordance with Hindu practice, but that night Sai Baba appeared to one of his devotees in a dream and requested that his body be buried in the temple, which was done. Sai Baba had promised his devotees that after leaving his body in 1918 he would remain active and vigorous in earthly matters, and several hundred thousand followers and visitors still come annually to his shrine at Shirdi in India.

Transforming Barren Ground Into A Spring That Cures Millions

BERNADETTE SOUBIROUS (A.D. 1844-1879). France. Lourdes.

In 1858 in the town of Lourdes there lived an illiterate peasant girl, Bernadette, at that time age 14. On Thursday, February 11, she accompanied her sister Marie and the sisters' playmate Jeanne Abadie to gather firewood sticks along the banks of the Gave River. Reaching the suburbs of Lourdes and arriving at a mill race near a shallow cave or grotto in a nearby mountainside the two companions crossed over. Bernadette planned to follow but paused long enough to remove her shoes and stockings. As she did, though it was a calm day, a great and startling wind arose, and shortly she found herself looking toward a briar bush growing beneath the cave's mouth. The bush made agitated or otherwise unusual movements, a cloud appeared above it, and above the cloud was a youthful and beautiful woman wearing a white robe with a blue sash around her waist. On her otherwise bare feet were gold-colored rosettes, and in her hands a rosary of white beads strung on a golden chain. With a gracious smile she beckoned Bernadette to her, and as Bernadette went to her she began reciting her own beads. Bernadette then fell to her knees praying, a position in which her returning companions found her. They themselves did not see the white-robed woman but instead saw nothing more spectacular than Bernadette's enraptured gaze, and so they laughed at her and headed her home. Here they treated the experience as the girl's imagination and forbade her return to

Bernadette Soubirous.

the grotto.

On February 14, however, the following Sunday, her family did permit the teen-ager in the company of a few children of her own age to revisit the grotto. She saw the same white-robed woman again, and the young girl's ecstatic appearance amazed and alarmed her companions who saw only Bernadette. After this second experience, the grotto again was put off limits to Bernadette until a few town ladies spurred by curiosity returned her there on February 18.

Left: The Statue at the Grotto. Right: Gabriel Garcam was paralyzed from the waist down and weighed only 78 pounds as an adult prior to his Lourdes cure that restored him, as shown here.

The white-robed lady appeared a third time, again only to the young girl, and asked her to return here daily for a fortnight. Bernadette agreed, and on the following three days (Friday, Saturday, and Sunday) had similar meetings with the mysterious lady, except by now before ever-increasing crowds. The curious bystanders still could not see the woman but were impressed by the ecstatic expression on the teen-ager's face. Though Bernadette returned to the grotto during the following three days and saw nothing, on February 24 the lady reappeared and commanded Bernadette to dig a hole in the dry ground at the grotto's entrance. This she dug with her hands, and from the once-dry earth a spring sprouted, gradually increasing in volume to about 33,000 gallons a day.

On February 26 Bernadette again saw the white-robed woman, and on the 27th the woman ordered the girl to "go and tell the priests to build a chapel" at the site. On February 28 the spectacle occurred before a Sunday crowd of more than 2,000 who still saw only Bernadette and not the white-robed woman. It occurred again the following two days but did not occur again from March 3 to March 25. On one of those unspectacular days, the 15th day on which the girl had promised to visit the grotto, there came a disappointed crowd of 15,000 onlookers. But on March 25 (feast of the Annunciation) the mysterious lady reappeared and this time replied to Bernadette's question that, yes, "I am the Immaculate Conception." Twelve days passed without the lady reappearing, but on April 7 she appeared again and three months later, July 16, she appeared for the 18th and last time. Soon afterwards Bernadette went to live with the Hospital Sisters established in the town, at age 22 she went to live in the convent at Nevers, and she died at age 35. Though Bernadette never had any other supernatural experiences her fame spread in like manner to that of the famous spring.

Among the throngs that have flocked to the spring, pilgrims on special occasions numbering between 50,000 and 100,000, there have been reported many hundreds of thousands of physical as well as spiritual healings. There is a procession of the Blessed Sacrament as the afflicted gather in a beautiful park and report miracles ranging from the spiritual to the reshaping of deformed babies and the curing of adults who for various reasons may have been given up medically as dead. The experience of an illiterate peasant girl led to the fame of the world's best-known healing spring.

Unifying The Invisible

MYRTLE PAGE FILLMORE (A.D. August 6, 1845-October 6, 1931). U.S.A. Ohio. Pagetown.

CHARLES FILLMORE (A.D. August 22, 1854-July 5, 1948). U.S.A. Minnesota. Indian Reservation outside small town of St. Cloud.

The Unity movement, headquartered at the Unity School of Christianity in Unity Village, Missouri, developed from the union of a husband-and-wife team. A supernatural experience that forever changed the couple's lives occurred in their middle age in Kansas City, Missouri.

Myrtle Page had been born eighth of nine children in the family of Marcus and Lucy Page of Pagetown, Ohio, an influential family whose forebears had settled Pagetown. As stalwart community leaders and as members of the Methodist Episcopal Church, this respectable family frowned upon most amusements, including card playing and dancing. A well-educated girl, Myrtle became a teacher, and because of poor health, including tuberculosis and malaria, accepted a teaching position in warmer and drier Denison, Texas.

Charles Fillmore, though his father was second cousin of United States president Millard Fillmore, was born into a family of meager circumstances, the older of two brothers. His father was an itinerant Indian trader on a small reservation near St. Cloud, Minnesota. When Charles was two years old and alone with his mother in their cabin, a band of Sioux Indians led by a medicine man tore the youth from his mother's arms, rode away with him for a day, and, after a ceremony which Charles vaguely remembers as mystical, returned him to his mother's cabin. Other than that possible mystical ceremony he had no

166

such religious experience as a youth, and their isolated life made formal church attendance impossible. When Charles was seven his father left home, building a cabin about 10 miles distant, and Charles and his younger brother Norton shared their time between their mother's and their father's cabins. After five years of this the younger brother, Norton, ran away and never returned to live with them, disappearing into the west except for a few perfunctory contacts with the family.

Soon after his younger brother's disappearance, Charles Fillmore dislocated his hip in a skating accident that would change his life. Despite or because of medical treatment that included six artificially produced sores on his leg to draw out the diseased condition, the leg injury grew more and more serious. Within two years the hip pocket had been destroyed, his withered leg had stopped growing, and Charles was hobbling about on handmade crutches. A crippled son was an added burden in the cabin environment, so Charles left home to earn money for his mother and himself. His search for better work took him first to a printing shop in St. Cloud, then further and further from home until he ended in Denison, Texas, working as a railroad clerk. There two important things happened to him. He was able to send for his mother, and he met schoolteacher Myrtle Page.

Despite his formal education limited to a few years in a Minnesota log cabin school, Charles Fillmore had developed a voracious appetite for reading. He and the attractive though sickly schoolteacher developed an increasing attraction for each other. They married on March 29, 1881, and that night left by train for Colorado, one of several states in which Charles meanwhile had explored livelihood opportunities. After finding no meaningful employment in other parts of Colorado, he arrived in Pueblo with 10 cents in his pocket. There, however, he prospered enough in real estate to support his family, including two sons born in Pueblo, in 1882 Lowel Page and in 1884 Waldo Rickert. But after his preliminary success the West did not prove financially stable for the Fillmores; for example, the real estate business dwindled and a silver mining venture failed. With things so bad there, the family looked east.

In 1884 Kansas City, Missouri, was a premier real estate area, with real estate transactions there about to exceed the value of those in Chicago. With his real estate experience in mind, Charles brought his family east to Kansas City in 1884. Here he learned that given the right conditions he could prosper exceedingly as a Kansas City realtor. One of his real estate successes was a subdivision named Gladstone Heights, the name it still bears.

In 1886, however, the fortunes of the Fillmores in Kansas City plummeted. In addition to the collapse of the Kansas City real estate boom, Myrtle had contracted malaria and her tuberculosis was worsening to the extent that doctors gave her only a short time to live. They advised that it was at least worth a try for her to travel elsewhere to look for a better climate. Again the West beckoned, but this time instead of "a dream of the West" a "dream of Kansas City" interfered. As related by Charles Fillmore, "I had a strange dream. An unseen voice said, 'Follow me.' I was led up and down the hilly streets of Kansas City . . . the Presence stopped and said . . . 'the invisible power that has located you will continue to be with you and aid you in the appointed work.'" The dream fell on fertile soil. Though their background had been one of serious hardships and his childhood had offered little opportunity for formal religious worship, his mother had lived an exemplary life as a firm Episcopalian believer. And much of the voracious reading accomplished by Charles had involved metaphysics, as would be exemplified by a future article about Shakespeare's metaphysics. He also would write that he and his wife had taken "more than forty courses (in metaphysical subjects) some of them costing as much as $100."

To Kansas City at this time of crisis in the Fillmore lives came a lecturer, Dr. E. B. Weeks. He represented the Illinois Metaphysical College founded by Emma Curtis Hopkins, disenchanted former associate of Mary Baker Eddy and Christian Science. With the Fillmore fortunes at such ebb, and Myrtle's fading health, the couple followed the recommendation of a friend who felt that their attending a Dr. Weeks' lecture might enhance Myrtle's life. It did, and, in fact, the supernatural event that night forever changed the couple's lives, but at first visibly affected only Myrtle. While Charles Fillmore came away from that lecture voicing no different attitude than when he went in, Myrtle Fillmore came away declaring that she felt new, a different, a transforming conviction blazing in her heart and mind. As she departed the hall one statement in the lecture kept coming again and again to mind: "I am a child of God and therefore I do not inherit sickness."

As Myrtle Fillmore pondered the lecturer's reassuring words, expecially that one sentence, her attitude began to change, her health changed, and eventually there would be a change in millions of lives throughout the world. In two years Myrtle Fillmore no longer was an invalid. She credited her faith in the healing teachings of the Bible, Jesus Christ, and God as making her absolutely whole. When her neighbors and other friends saw the change in her and heard her explanation of the miracle, people began to come to her for help.

From across the street a crippled neighbor came on crutches. She prayed with the man and repeatedly reassured him that because he was a child of God he had not inherited his condition and that God had commanded him to be perfect. His healing was complete. A boy's eyes had such severe cataracts they resembled the whites of eggs. Myrtle Fillmore talked with the child, they prayed together, and he was completely healed.

Her love for those who came was so obvious that this seemed to put people in the right frame of mind, even before she started talking with them. She stayed up into the late hours of the night thinking only of helping them, charging no one for her long hours of serving them. She did not try to rationalize what was happening. She simply prayed with people, she talked with them, she told them how she had been healed, and they were healed. She did not try to concentrate on understanding why it was she was able to help people get healed. She was too busy working successfully with them, and her fame began spreading across the countryside.

Meanwhile Charles Fillmore was taking an opposite approach to that of his wife. He was what is known in the business world as a "hard sell." Not only did he consider himself a hard-headed businessman, he had a family to support. True, he had seen his wife's healing, and then every day the miracles in the lives of others. And after that Presence first appeared to him in a dream, subsequent dreams became more and more vivid until he found himself being able to predict with accuracy more and more future events. But whereas his wife had seemed to be able

Charles Fillmore.

at once to understand the lecturer's words, and despite his increasing clairvoyance, he found that he had to continue as always to analyze and study before jumping. An intelligent and practical man, he began seeking more and more reasons for what his physical eyes and his dreams were showing him in his own home. He decided that his reading, though vast in the past, had only scratched the surface. He began reading all the books he could find even remotely concerned with supernatural power in everyday life; and also, as they became available, he enrolled in local and correspondence courses on the subject. He and Myrtle even went briefly to Chicago to study under Emma Curtis Hopkins.

The result of the practical experience and study by Myrtle and Charles Fillmore was the founding of the Unity School of Christianity, headquartered at a beautiful 1,400-acre spiritual

Myrtle Fillmore.

and recreational retreat at Unity Village, Missouri. From prayer and study and from practical application, the Fillmores decided that people can learn to see themselves and others as God's children, instead of seeing their defects and shortcomings and that —to put it in rough vernacular—"what they see is what they get." They named their program Unity, quoting the Bible verse, "The Spirit that is in me is in you."

They established *Wee Wisdom* magazine, the oldest children's magazine in America, today with a circulation of many thousand. It is published in Braille for blind children and distributed to them free of charge. It does not attempt to preach, and many parents, teachers, and children do not even class it as a religious publication. Yet the Christian philosophy is in each issue, and the Fillmores credit its success entirely to prayer. As Charles Fillmore wrote, "If God ever did answer prayer, He always does, being the same God. Therefore, if there seems to be any lack of principle, it is in the one who prays. Misunderstanding of the will and nature of our God prevents prayer from being answered.''

Today almost 200 million pieces of mail pour out from Unity School each year. There are three English language magazines: *UNITY, Daily World*, and *Wee Wisdom*, with approximately two million subscribers to these magazines. *Daily World* is published in eight languages, the Spanish edition, for example, going to 50,000 subscribers. Each issue of each magazine promotes what the Fillmores called the use of affirmations and denials, spiritual decrees rather than petitions in addressing God. Charles Fillmore taught that God is law; that life is governed by law, every incident in life; and that as we gain an understanding of the divine law, we can use it to change our life. He taught that, "Affirmations and denials are statements that deny the reality of undesirable conditions and affirm the reality of God and His good, such as: *'There is nothing in all the universe for me to fear, for greater is He that is in me than he that is in all the world, for I am a radiant, all wise, all-loving, all-conquering son of God.'*"

The hundreds of thousands of spiritual healings that have been part of the Unity movement do not form a new concept, of course, but the movement has been innovative in a major way. It not only promoted the so-called power of positive thinking a generation before the concept became generally popular, it went a step further in the matter of spiritual and physical healing and promotion of material success. Though the Fillmores agreed that the matter of healing by "laying on of hands" had Biblical antecedent and seemed to work best for some healers, because God is omniscient it should be as easy to heal without regard to distance between the healer and the subject. The result has become known as Silent Unity. If one arrives at Unity Village day or night there can be seen a light shining from one of the rooms in the Silent Unity Building where telephone operators remain on duty day and night answering approximately a half-million telephone calls annually that come from all around the world. There is a toll-free number, especially convenient for the great many distraught callers who have been involved in accidents or otherwise are unable to locate change for emergency

172

calls. Unity personnel bless each call as it is received, as they do with each of the more than one-million pieces of mail received annually.

In the final analysis perhaps one of the greatest events at Unity was the life and eternal aspirations of Charles Fillmore himself. His short, withered leg continued to heal until it was almost whole by the time of his death. What is more, the same audacious personality that earlier had placed him in "boom and bust" situations in various parts of the country found him in the latter part of his life determined to live forever in his present bodily form. Time and again he began quoting Jesus' promise, "If a man keep my word, he shall never see death." When friends advised him that if in fact he should one day die physically, as seemed likely, his oft-publicized statements about living forever would cast disrepute upon his other accomplishments with Unity. But, with the good-humored optimism for which he was known, he would toss aside such fears. A short time before his death at age 94 he was approached with the suggestion that he get together some biographical material about himself. "Wait another hundred years," was his reply.

He wrote that death is the "last enemy, whom we have resolved finally to overcome, as taught by Jesus." He reminded others that Paul taught, "Be transformed by the renewal of your mind." He would reaffirm that the way for a person to change a physical condition is to change his thinking. "The purpose of prayer is to change your thinking. His will is always, only good. All that keeps you from your good is your failure to unify yourself in thought with the Source of all good, God." He reminded others not to think about the problem, but about God. And that Jesus taught, "And whatever you ask in prayer, you will receive, if you have faith." He said that what he was advocating was a return to Christ's original teachings, a return needed for centuries. In answer to the question if he really expected to live forever he replied, "This question is often asked . . . . Some of them seem to think that I am either a fanatic or a joker if I take myself seriously in the hope that I shall with Jesus attain eternal life in the body. But the fact is that I am very serious about the matter . . . . It seems to me that someone should have initiative enough to make at least an attempt to raise his body to the Jesus Christ consciousness. Because none of the followers of Jesus has attained the victory over this terror of humanity does not prove that it cannot be done . . . . I do not claim that I have yet attained that perfection but I am on the way. My leg is still out of joint but it is improving as I continue to work under the direction and guidance of Spirit."

For a while it seemed that Charles Fillmore intended to prove, no matter what, that others were wrong and he was right. On October 6, 1931, Myrtle Fillmore died. On December 31, 1933, at age 79 he married Cora G. Dedrick, for many years private secretary to the Fillmores and at one time director of Silent Unity. That same month, after more than 40 years of continuous service, he retired from the pulpit of the Unity Society of Practical Christianity in Kansas City to dedicate his life to nationwide lecture tours accompanied by his new bride. In his eighties he started taking singing lessons. As his crippled leg improved, he threatened to start taking dancing lessons. Acquaintances pointed out that at age 94 his handwriting was a vigorous as a young man's. In February of 1948 he still was making speeches at Unity centers in Los Angeles.

However, in April of 1948 Charles Fillmore returned to his home near Unity Village and from then on slowly began to slip away. He showed no fear of death. "I am facing it, but I am not afraid of it," he would remark. When a friend came into the room he told him twice that in his opinion the most important words in the world are, "Christ in you, the hope of glory." Several days before he died he said, "I am going to have a new body, anyway, and this time it's going to be a perfect body." Shortly before death he began to have a recurring vision. "Do you see it?" he would ask, staring intently upward. "The new Jerusalem, coming down from God, the new heaven and the new earth—don't you see it?"

Charles Fillmore died on July 5, 1948. Fillmore children and other relatives helped carry on the Unity work. Today the movement continues under the direction of Charles and Myrtle Fillmore's grandson, Charles Rickert Fillmore. The Unity movement continues to exemplify its unity of family as it does unity worldwide. (An interesting inside view of Unity, written by a professional on the inside, is *The Story of Unity,* James Dillet Freeman, Unity Books, 1978.)

Visiting "Lord Of Heaven" Leads To 10,000 Temples

OMIKI SAN MAEKAWA (A.D. June 2, 1798-January 26, 1887). Japan. Sammaiden in the province of Yamato.

She was a daughter of the prosperous farming family Maekawa, influential in the community, with male members permitted to carry Samurai swords. At her birth an auspicious cloud of five colors hovered over the home to the amazement of the villagers. The family gave the little girl the personal name of Miki, which she carried the remainder of her life. She was of delicate health, an affectionate and kind-hearted girl who made a reputation for herself because of deeds of kindness to neighboring children. Born 23 years before the birth of Christian Scientist founder Mary Baker Eddy in the United States, Miki later as a religious leader often would be compared with Mary Baker Eddy, and her religious movement compared with Christian Science.

Maekawa family members were devout followers of the Jodo sect of Buddhism, and while yet a child Miki decided to become a nun. Considerations of two Japanese families intervened. Her family and a neighboring family of wealthy farmers named Zambei decided on an interfamily marriage. The 23-year-old Zambei son Nakayama married 12-year-old Miki. The girl first insisted, however, that she be free in marriage to conduct morning and evening services to Buddha at the home altar.

During her long marriage Miki gave birth to six children, five daughters and one son, though two of the daughters died in early childhood. It was after 28 years of marriage, on December 9, 1838, that Miki became convinced that God had taken possession of her to reveal himself through her and save the world. Her son was suffering acutely from chronic pains in the feet; her husband was suffering with a severe eye ailment; and she was sick with a stomach problem, perhaps colic. To treat the sick, the family called in as a medium an ascetic Buddhist priest, and while assisting the priest in his healing work the mother became transfigured by the glory of God and a great dignity settled upon her. From out of her a voice spoke these words to those around her: "I am the Lord of Heaven. I am the original and true God who has come down from heaven to save the whole world." Miki's transfigured state continued for three days after which father, mother, and son immediately were healed of their infirmities.

As a result of meeting the Lord of Heaven, Miki began a life as a god-possessed saint, living in this world but not altogether of it. She gave away all her possessions and proceeded upon a massive campaign of healing the sick. Her movement resulted in the Tenri-Kyo doctrine, "the religion of Heavenly Wisdom," best known of numerous new sects in Japan showing Shinto and to a lesser extent Buddhist and Christian influence.

Though China played an important role in bringing Shinto and Buddhist religions into Japan, the two religions have distinct Japanese characteristics. The name Shinto originates with the Chinese word Shen-Tao, the Tao and Way of the Gods. In correct Japanese the word Kami either means gods or some other type of divine power such as manifested, for example, in peculiarly twisted trees or huge rocks or some other powerful manifestation of nature. The account of the Shinto gods is collected in the *Nihongi*, or *Chronicles of Japan*. Though these are lists of names and historic stories rather than devotional readings, from among these names of ancient deities two became preeminent and led to modern Japanese worship. These two overriding gods gave birth to the islands of Japan and many other gods and in the chronicles have the god names "Male-who-invites" and "Female-who-invites."

The leader Miki advocated less formal religion than represented by these elaborate temples for which Japan is best known.

176

The offspring of these two gods is a chief deity called the sun goddess, Amaterasu Omi-Kami, the "Heaven-illuminating goddess." She was a benevolent ruler of both day and daylight, ruling wisely and justly amid peace and plenty. But her brother, Susa-no-wo, "Swift Impetuous," the storm god, attacked. Amaterasu found haven in a cave, pulling light into the cave with her, thus plunging the outside into darkness. Gods disliking darkness assembled outside the mouth of the cave and danced and chanted charms in order to get her to return outside with light. They hung a mirror on a tree. When she looked out and saw her beautiful image in the mirror she reached for it thus enabling the gods to pull her out of the cave and return light to the heavens. Though the gods banished Susa-no-wo, his followers resisted the sun goddess until a compromise gave Susa-no-wo "domain of the invisible" and with it powers that included magic and omens. Today he is petitioned at times of pestilence or drought or other disaster, and his shrine at Izumo on Japan's northern coast is Japan's second greatest.

The greatest shrine in Japan is at Ise', to Amaterasu herself, who continues to be chief of the Shinto gods. Here in addition to imperial paraphenalia are kept a mirror, a sword, and a bead, all believed to have been passed down from her.

To rule over the Japanese islands Amaterasu sent her son Ni-ni-gi. He and the daughter of Mount Fuji married, and their grandson, Jimmu Tenno, became Japan's first emperor. Thus Japan's earthly emperors, starting with Jimmu Tenno, descended from the goddess Amaterasu and since the tenth century have been called the Mikado. Though other great Japanese families claim descent from lesser gods, only the emperors can claim descent from the great goddess Amaterasu.

In addition to Amaterasu there are many lesser gods (kami) in Japan. Some estimates cite the number at 800,000. There are spirits of trees, food, wind, rain, storms, earthquakes, as well as the family, and many other categories. No massive stone temples or pagodas are associated with the Shinto religion in Japan, purity and simplicity marking these shrines. These contrast with the elaborate Buddhist sanctuaries that reflect China's great influence throughout Japanese life, both spiritual and secular. Leading to the Shinto sanctuary always is one or more ceremonial gateways, succeeded by a tree-lined lane to a simple wooden sanctuary itself.

The utilitarian aspect of Shintoism aligns itself readily with Miki's religion of Tenri-kyo, emphasizing as it does the combating of sickness, poverty, and strife. Today its 4,000,000 followers worship in an estimated 10,000 temples. At Tenri, center of Tenri-kyo, are large temples, and the movement has constructed massive communal edifices. It is said that the "Lord of Heaven's" request to Miki to give away all her goods has led not only to spiritual blessings but to a religion that leads toward material success on earth. (For a scholarly coverage of the Tenri-kyo movement read *The National Faiths of Japan; A Study in Modern Shinto*, D. C. Holtom, Paragon Book Reprint Corporation, 1965.)

Beautiful temples such as this are commonplace in Japan where there are thousands of temples and an estimated 800,000 gods.

Visitors From Other Worlds Change This One

JOAN OF ARC (A.D. January 6, 1412-May 30, 1431). France. Domremy.

The village home of the peasant farming couple Jacques and Isabelle d'Arc was as primitive as the others dotting the small French town of Domremy. Yet this primitive house had a bit more status. Jacques was the third highest ranking citizen in town, immediately after the mayor and the sheriff. To this respectable solid French peasant family of devout Catholic faith, Jeanne, known popularly as Joan, was born the second daughter and the fourth child.

This strong and versatile peasant girl developed muscles as she helped with the farm chores, including shepherding the cattle and sheep, as did the other peasant children. At times she and other children sang and danced around a tree in the woods known as the "Fairy Tree."

In one way, though, she was not typical. Sometimes when her parents believed her to be in the meadows tending the flocks or playing with other children, she would take a long hike through more distant fields and woods past a spring and on up a hill to a clearing. Here waited an isolated, tiny, unpretentious chapel, the shrine of Our Lady of Bermont. There Joan worshipped in the manner of other devout Catholics who came in more routine ways, perhaps paying special veneration to a crude wooden statue of Notre Dame de Bermont. Far more unusual, however, than a devout lass slipping away from work and play were some amazing, unexpected visitations from other worlds. Joan of Arc began encountering bright lights and visitors seen only by herself.

It all started in 1424 when Joan was 12. As reported in a contemporary letter to the duke of Milan, some girl companions, playing nearby as Joan tended her parents' sheep, invited her to join them in a race, perhaps for a prize of a handful of flowers. Whereupon Joan ran the course with such speed that one of the girls cried out, "Joan, I see you flying above the ground. . . ." When Joan arrived, or landed as the case might be, at the end of the race she was described as "rapt and deprived of her senses." Then as Joan was en route between her house and the meadows, "suddenly a luminous cloud appeared before her eyes, and out of the cloud came a voice, saying, 'Joan, you are destined to lead a different kind of life and to accomplish miraculous things, for you are she who has been chosen by the King of Heaven to restore the Kingdom of France, and to aid and protect King Charles, who has been driven from his domains. You shall put on masculine clothes, you shall bear arms and become the head of the army; all things shall be guided by your counsel.' After these words had been spoken, the cloud vanished, and the girl, astounded by such a marvel, at first could not give credence to it, but, in her ignorant innocence, remained perplexed as to whether she should believe it or not. Night and day similar visions appeared to her, renewing and repeating their words. She kept her own counsel; to none . . . did she speak; and in this perplexity she continued for the space of five years."

A briefer description came from Joan herself. Testifying at her own trial seven years later at age 19, just before being burned alive at the stake, she gave this succinct, poignant account of that first of many thousands of strange encounters: "I was in my thirteenth year (age 12) when God sent a voice to guide me. At first, I was very much frightened. The voice came towards the hour of noon, in summer, in my father's garden. I had fasted the preceding day. I heard the voice on my right hand, in the direction of the church. I seldom hear it without [seeing] a light. That light always appears on the side from which I hear the voice."

Once she heard that first voice she heard it or others every day with increasing clarity for the rest of her life. At first she was frightened and wondered if what she had seen and heard actually could be real. Then, after she had seen and listened to her first amazing visitor several times, she decided that she recognized him at last because, as she would inform her judges at her trial, "he spoke with the tongues of angels." She decided that the identity of her visitor was none other than Saint Michael. She became absolutely convinced following a number of such visits, especially after "Saint Michael taught me and showed me so many things." At this definite conclusion, any lingering fear and doubt left her for an unshakable trust that lasted throughout her life. In one of their daily conversations, Saint Michael explained to her that Saint Catherine and Saint Margaret soon would appear to her and that since they would be sent by the Lord, she must obey their instructions. Though Joan listened with care she still told no one.

Meanwhile the three saints, Michael, Margaret, and Catherine, appeared to Joan routinely. In addition to those three, she also saw the Archangel Gabriel and several hundred other angels, but the regulars were those three who first came to her attention. The bright light always accompanied their arrival.

Asked at her trial whether their hair was short or long she replied that she did not know and, to the judges' surprise, she could not say whether they had arms or other limbs. Saint Michael had wings, she explained, but she refused to say about the bodies or limbs of Catherine and Margaret. When they asked her what she meant by this refusal, she responded that she had already told them what she knew and intended to say nothing further. She explained that she already had said as much as she felt that her three mysterious visitors wanted her to say. She added with spirit that she would rather have her throat cut than tell everything she knew, unless it concerned the trial. She indicated that when she and they had approached each other, she would fall on her knees and embrace them. Asked whether she had felt their warmth when she embraced them, she replied that she scarcely could embrace them without feeling and touching them.

Also in response to a question at her trial Joan would explain that her visitors spoke to her in French, and she would ask her judges why they should have spoken to her in English when they were not on the English side. Though they smelled good and wore beautiful crowns, she either could not or would not

182

describe their clothes. She said that they spoke well and beautifully with soft and humble voices. Other witnesses reported that if Joan was in the fields and church bells rang out she would make the sign of the cross and bend her knees. It was reported after her death that she had heard her voices most distinctively during the ringing of those church bells. Whatever time of day she had seen and heard one or more of her saints, she was positive she had done so daily, totaling hundreds of times across a span of seven years. She explained that though her eyes had seen the light and the three visitors many times, in those eyes were tears after they left because she had wanted them to take her away with them.

About two years after Joan began receiving visits from other worlds, usually in the daytime, her father at nighttime began having his own supernatural experiences. Uninformed by Joan of her own amazing experiences, he began having ominous dreams during which he learned that his daughter would go away with soldiers. The only logical explanation was that he was being informed that his virtuous daughter was about to lose her virtue, and, of course, this upset him. It unnerved him so much, in fact, he did not mention the revelation to Joan, but instead warned his wife of his fears, and she then passed them on to the girl. As a result, both parental guidance and observations of the girl were tightened. Jacques d'Arc did talk to his sons about it, the father perhaps intending the conversation to thereby reach Joan and be an even greater warning. Her father capped his warning through his sons thusly: "If I believed that the thing I dreamed about her should come to pass, I should want you to drown her; and if you did not do so, I would drown her myself." Thus a strict Catholic father of the fifteenth century felt that the death of his daughter was preferable to loss of her virtue.

Everything considered, Joan's family was becoming less and less typical. The visitors were communicating with Joan in person and with her father through dreams, but father and daughter were not telling each other. She was the only one in her family who knew of her visitors. But in a round-about-way she was learning that her father's dreams were describing to him the same future role the visitors described to her.

Joan's saintly visitors were becoming more and more insistent that she go help King Charles VII of France. It was the last decades of the Hundred Years' War between France and England that had begun in 1337. For the better part of a hundred years in that war the kings of England had tried to unite France and England under one crown—the crown of England. Now the military predicament of King Charles and his French supporters was growing more and more desperate. His own mother had insinuated that her weakling son Charles VII was illegitimate, an accusation not intended to bolster her son's claim to the crown of all France. In October 1428 the English put Orleans under seige. The prodding of Joan's saints grew more and more persistent. But Joan resisted, saying to her saints, "I am a poor girl, I do not know how to ride or fight." The saints were not swayed: "It is God who commands it."

Yielding at last in January of 1429, Joan, then aged 17, left Domremy never to return. Still without revealing her mission to her family or anyone else she went to the nearby town of Vaucouleurs, less than a day's hike, and presented herself to King Charles' commander in that town. She asked the amazed commander to either take her or send her under escort to King Charles at Chinon, some 350 miles distance across a countryside in a state of war. The skeptical commander's reluctance was understandable. At last Joan told him about her amazing visitations, the first man she told before she told the king. The skeptical commander brought a priest to interrogate Joan. She told them both, "Have you not heard the prophecy, that France shall be lost through a woman [the king's mother who was siding with the English] and shall be redeemed by a virgin from the frontiers of Lorraine?" She was persuasive. On February 17, 1429, through clairvoyance, she announced in the town of Vaucouleurs that the French army had suffered a great defeat in a battle near Orleans. When this was confirmed a few days later her credibility rose sharply.

At last the commander dispatched a petition to the king. The king replied in the affirmative, and on February 23, 1429, Joan of Arc, mounted with her escort of six men, began the 350-mile perilous ride across France. Joan was dressed as a man, perhaps as a camouflage. For security they sometimes traveled at night and reportedly muffled their horses' hooves. Although from time to time members of her escort openly showed their skepticism, she reassured them that her brothers in Paradise, and God Himself, had already informed her that she must go to war in order to recover the kingdom.

She traveled with the same endurance as her escort, bothering them only by her constant desire to hear Mass. "If only we could hear Mass, " she said, "all would be well." But her fame already was spreading, and afraid she might be recognized, they provided her the opportunity to attend Mass only twice during their 11-day journey. Over the years a number of historians have had sport debating why Joan maintained her virginity, even though heaven-sent, as she slept among the group of rough soldiers during the long journey. Because no contemporary portrait of Joan of Arc is known to exist, some have conjectured that Joan's looks and her masculine clothes, worn day and night, saved her from the soldiers. But members of her group testified later that her demeanor, attitude, and mission spared her from even their lewd thoughts.

Yet Joan of Arc, whether beautiful or less than beautiful, was a woman in a bawdy era and area, and greeting her arrival as she approached the king's castle in Chinon was a bawdy event that ended supernaturally. Joan had to make her way up a steep hill and across a main drawbridge before reaching the castle for audience with the king. As she was preparing to enter the castle a horseman halted her steed to stare at her and exclaim, "Jarnidieu! Is that not the Pucelle [for *Maid*, the French name by which she was becoming famous]? If I could have her for one night, I would not return her in like condition." Joan heard his words. "Ha!" she told him, "In the name of God, you deny Him, and you so near to your death!" Within an hour he fell into water and drowned as Joan meanwhile proceeded to the meeting with her king in a huge castle reception room containing more than 300 people. The capricious king, whose father had been insane, pulled a trick on the masculine-garbed Joan by concealing himself among the crowd, dressed in clothes like some of his lords. Joan, requesting aloud that they not attempt to mislead her, went straight to the disguised king, curtsied, and then told him: "The King of Heaven sends me to you with the message that you shall be anointed and crowned in the city of Reims, and that you shall be the lieutenant of the King of Heaven, who is the King of France."

Joan of Arc's home town of Domremy, France, remains this sleepy farmland village that she knew five centuries ago.

Though already a convincing demonstration, the king prolonged his attempted disguise. "It is not I who am the king, Jeanne." He pointed to one of his lords. "*There* is the king." But still refusing to be misled, she replied, "In God's name, noble prince, it is you and none other." To further convince him she asked him to step aside so that she could tell him things in secret. He did, and when she told him very secret things about his personal life, including the fact that indeed he was legitimate, concerning which of course she could have had no natural knowledge, the large crowd saw conviction in his exalted demeanor. But when she asked the vacillating king to provide her with an army that she could lead to save the city of Orleans from its seige by the English, he subjected her to a protracted series of additional tests. Some of the top clergy of France, including university professors, were summoned to interrogate her concerning the bright lights, saints, and angels she kept reporting in her company. Even as precious weeks were being lost to the English, the king had women examine the girl intimately to report back to him whether or not Joan was a man or woman and, if a woman, whether she was in fact the widely publicized virgin of Domremy.

Satisfied at last, King Charles VII acquiesced to the audacious proposal of Joan of Arc that she be allowed to dispatch a
letter to the king of England, warning the English either to leave
France or be prepared to suffer the consequences. ". . . deliver
the keys of all the good towns you have taken and violated in
France to the Maid (Pucelle) who has been sent by God the
King of Heaven. . . . Go away, for God's sake, back to your own
country; otherwise, await news of the Maid, who will soon visit
you to your detriment."

The English reaction to this letter from a peasant girl from
Domremy, France, was neither printable nor otherwise returned.
So King Charles VII of France outfitted Joan of Arc with
armour, banners, and a horse. On the banner was a representa-
tion of two angels plus a portrait of Jesus and the words JHE-
SUS MARIA. She refused the king's offer of a sword and instead requested that a letter be sent to the clergy in another
town who would find, according to Joan's supernatural voices, a
sword buried in the ground behind an altar in a certain church.
The church people there found the sword, and though it was
very rusty, as soon as they started to clean it the rust fell off
without any difficulty. Local clergy were so impressed they sent
her a sheath along with the sword.

On April 27, 1429, Joan of Arc proceeded toward Orleans
leading an army of 3,000 to 4,000 soldiers. Many supernatural
events occurred as she first freed Orleans from English control
and then one French town after another. As a result of a sudden
change of wind, Joan's forces successfully crossed a river, an important prelude to the saving of Orleans. Joan publicly prophesied that she would be wounded in the breast, which she was,
and then later in the thigh, which she was. She asked a soldier
to step away from a seemingly safe area, and as soon as he had
done so a projectile landed where he had stood. The English
made unrealistic self-defeating military decisions as Joan's
voices on the other hand directed her armies to the right places
at the right time. King Charles VII was anointed and crowned in
the city of Reims as she had predicted, and she stood at the
ceremony beside her king in a position never granted even to
the greatest peers of France. All this had occurred less than five
months after she left Domremy.

Yet, with the crowning of the king, Joan's unrelenting, always accurate guidance from her visitors from other worlds seemed to begin a gradual decline. To her dismay and shock the voices told her that she had less than a year to live. In a minor skirmish with the English during a foray that had no real purpose, a kind of battle situation that normally she could have directed with ease, the small force with her was defeated and she was captured. After her capture and before her trial, she made one of the most spectacular jumps in history. From the top of her prison tower, estimated to be at least 60 or 70 feet high, she leaped to the ground without breaking any bones. Although she soon was in custody again, her leap at once brought to mind the account of her flying above the ground the first day of her visit from other worlds. Leading clergy in the Catholic Church considered Joan a witch, a sorceress, and a heretic. It seemed natural that the church should have first chance at her, and so the English turned her over for trial. During a protracted trial in the town of Rouen, still under English control, she was interrogated by some of the highest ranking clergy in the Catholic church, as she had been earlier at the instigation of King Charles VII in the area of Chinon. Though she had passed that first test to the satisfaction of King Charles, the capricious and ungrateful king did nothing to help her in this one. Week after week the judges interrogated her about the light, the saints, the angels, and her masculine mode of dress. She was asked to denounce all of that and save her life. But she replied that the voices requested otherwise.

The clergy turned her over to the secular, to English soldiers, for her burning at the stake. She was terrified of fire and asked to be beheaded. Her request was refused, but as she prayed for forgiveness for those executing her, an English soldier, convinced that she was saintly rather than of the devil as she was condemned, formed a crude cross of wood and handed it to her. Aloud she kept crying out the name of Jesus. It was the last word she was heard to say before her head sank forward in flames.

Supernatural events now became visible to the eyes of others. The name Jesus leapt written across the flames. A white dove flew out of the flames and headed in the direction of France. The executioner said that he was damned for having burnt a saint and that God would never forgive him. But he already had been forgiven by the best known person in French history, a girl who in 19 years became known throughout the world. Almost five centuries later the Catholic church on May 16, 1920, canonized Joan of Arc as a saint. (A fascinating and well-documented look at the amazing life of Joan of Arc is *Saint Joan of Arc*, V. Sackville—West Nicolson, The Literary Guild of New York, 1936.)

There is no known contemporary portrait of Joan Of Arc. This statue at her village, Domremy, France, is considered one of her truest representations.

World-Binding Broadcasting

**M.G. "PAT" ROBERTSON (A.D. March 29, 1930-   ).
U.S.A. Virginia. Lexington.**

Pat Robertson was born Marion Gordon Robertson, son of A. Willis Robertson, United States Senator from Virginia. He grew up amid affluence and enjoyed the best of life. At age 20, in 1950, he was graduated as a Phi Beta Kappa from Washington and Lee, then in 1955 earned a law degree from Yale Law School.

However, soon after graduation from Yale it became clear that an ordinary life of success was not enough for young Robertson. For starters, instead of practicing law he joined the Marine Corps from 1950-52, serving as a front-line marine combat officer in the Korean conflict. After the war he had difficulty adjusting. For a while he worked for the W. R. Grace Company in New York City as "a troubleshooter," but troubles within himself began to affect his value in solving company troubles. He drifted into other endeavors in New York, including partnership at one point in an electronics firm.

Then one day, Robertson says, God found him as an adult, and he was "born again." The newly dedicated Robertson turned from a possible career of law begun at Yale, from the troubled memories of the war, and from dabbling in first one endeavor and then another. He enrolled in New York Theological Seminary and while at the seminary began to realize that all the tributaries of his varied background should lead into the main channel of public broadcasting.

Television outlets throughout the world permit Dr. M. G. "Pat" Robertson, shown here, to be viewed by a greater populous than any other television personality in the world.

Dr. Robertson, after New York Theological Seminary, found that on a material level his electronics background helped give him the courage in 1961 to purchase a dilapidated UHF station in Portsmouth, Virginia. From that time on the ordained

Baptist minister has been involved in broadcasting with worldwide growth unparalleled in the broadcast industry. His multimillion-dollar Christian Broadcasting Network (CBN) today includes four owned and operated television stations, 200 television affiliates, six owned and operated radio stations, 150 radio affiliates, and a futuristic satellite delivery system. In addition to covering all 50 states in the United States, CBN reaches 20 foreign countries. More than 800 staff members operate this network with its potential worldwide viewing audience of more than a half-billion. CBN's best known program is its 60-minute and 90-minute "700 Club," a daily talk-variety show that got its name from 700 charter members who contributed $10 a month. The club's membership now has risen from the 700 to 600,000 members.

Dr. Robertson is a member of the Board of Directors of the National Religious Broadcasters and the United Virginia/Seaboard National Bank. He is president of three wholly owned CBN subsidiaries: First Colonial Corporation, Continental Pictures Corporation, and Continental Broadcasting Network. In 1977 at Virginia Beach, his network founded, under his chancellorship, CBN University, offering a Master of Arts degree in Communication. The doctor's many awards include the Distinguished Merit Citation from the National Conference of Christians and Jews, the FBI Award, and regional awards from as far away as a resolution by the California State Senate presenting him its Commendation Award. He is the author of the bestselling book *Shout It From The Housetops.*

Despite the fact that young Dr. Robertson has accomplished so much by age 50, he is best known by millions who have seen him daily along with cohost Ben Kinchlow praying for healing and other miracles worldwide. Theirs is the focal point for 83 on-the-site counseling centers worldwide, manned by 10,000 volunteer counselors who annually handle more than a million telephone calls from persons needing spiritual and physical help. Dr. "Pat" Robertson has found that even as all people on earth breathe air, all have similar problems that can be helped by means of the same medium. His worldwide supernatural healing programs over the airwaves, accompanied by reported hundreds of thousands of cures, are unsurpassed in broadcast history.

192